M000072918

My Tears in His Bottle

My Tears in His Bottle

Prayers from the Heart of
a Special Needs' Mom

By Pat Hays

Copyright © 2017 by Pat Hays.

ISBN: Hardcover   978-1-5434-2428-7
             Softcover   978-1-5434-2427-0
             eBook   978-1-5434-2429-4

All rights reserved. No part of this book may be reproduced or transmitted in
any form or by any means, electronic or mechanical, including photocopying,
recording, or by any information storage and retrieval system, without
permission in writing from the copyright owner.

Scripture quotations marked (NLT) are taken from the Holy Bible, New Living
Translation, copyright © 1996, 2004, 2007 by Tyndale House Foundation.
Used by permission of Tyndale House Publishers, Inc., Carol Stream, Illinois
60188. All rights reserved.

Scripture quotations marked NKJV are taken from the New King James
Version. Copyright © 1982 by Thomas Nelson, Inc. Used by permission. All
rights reserved.

Scripture quotations marked NASB are taken from the New American
Standard Bible®. Copyright © 1960, 1962, 1963, 1968, 1971, 1972, 1973,
1975, 1977, 1995 by The Lockman Foundation. Used by permission.

Scripture quotations marked NIV are taken from the Holy Bible, New
International Version®. NIV®. Copyright © 1973, 1978, 1984 by International
Bible Society. Used by permission of Zondervan. All rights reserved. [Biblica]

Any people depicted in stock imagery provided by Thinkstock are models,
and such images are being used for illustrative purposes only.
Certain stock imagery © Thinkstock.

Print information available on the last page.

Rev. date: 05/24/2017

To order additional copies of this book, contact:
Xlibris
1-888-795-4274
www.Xlibris.com
Orders@Xlibris.com
532464

For my sons, Nick and Will, God's perfect creations.

You keep track of all my sorrows. You have collected all my tears in your bottle. You have recorded each one in your book. Psalm 56:8 NLT

Foreword

The dictionary says objects are parallel when they extend in the same direction, are equal at all points, yet never converging or diverging. Parallel is getting close, but never connecting. In geometry, it is two straight lines lying in the same plane, but never meeting, no matter how far extended. In life, parallel means existing alongside others, but never having real relationships. I had never given this concept much thought until my life took a turn that forced me to understand parallel worlds. I am the mother of two sons on the autism spectrum. They have Asperger's Syndrome, also known as high-functioning autism.

I am firmly grounded in the world that most of us take for granted. We make connections with others. We express our feelings. We know what is and what is not socially acceptable. We know love, respect, honesty, and integrity and we have empathy for others. We have self-control and order in our lives. Autism is a different world with its own rules and viewpoints. So, in my life, there are two distinct worlds—the one I live in as the parent of autistic children and the world my children live in.

I am not satisfied to live parallel lives with my children, although I sometimes joke that I am living in a parallel universe where reality is suspended. I want to reach into their worlds and see things through their eyes. In order to do this, I have to stop and make a conscious effort to see the world through the same lens that they do. I want to connect with them. I am not content to just walk parallel to them. I long to understand what they are thinking and why, what makes them happy and sad. I want them to learn empathy and have good hearts. I want to reach into their world and grasp them and pull them as hard as I can into my world. As exhausting as it can be to parent an autistic child, I know I would have missed out on something special if I did not have these children.

I did not seek this path in life. God gave it to me. If it had been a choice, I doubt that I would have chosen it. This life requires much more patience, flexibility, and understanding than most of us have—me included. I summon my strength from the Lord. He never gives us more than we handle *with* His help. Yes, there are days when I want to give up and say, "I can't do this anymore." Then the next day dawns and God restores my faith in His plan and He places hope and peace in my heart. When I think He is gone, and I am walking alone, He comforts me and reminds me that I am wrapped safely and securely in His arms.

Autism is a long journey without a final destination. I can't imagine walking on this journey alone. God walks with me and He will walk with the thousands of other parents and families who share this experience. The chance that a child will be diagnosed with autism is one in every 68. This prevalence means there are a lot of families coping with the multitude of issues that come with an autism diagnosis such as trouble transitioning, sensory issues, arm and hand flapping, lack of social skills, and disruptive and aggressive behavior to name a few.

Families on this journey will find comfort in knowing that you are not traveling alone. There are thousands on this journey with us. We experience good times, but trying times seem to occur more frequently. You will find that heartache, tears, despair, anguish and pain are universal, just as joy, laughter, love, and hope exist. Remember that God knows all our sorrows and He collects all our tears in His bottle.

Father,

Please forgive me. At times, I have been so angry with You because my children have special needs. Sometimes I have felt cheated because I couldn't have biological children, so I adopted my sons. I had such high expectations about motherhood and what my life would be like. Instead, motherhood has been totally different than I could have ever imagined. I have often felt sorry for myself and wondered why things turned out as they did.

God, please forgive me because now I can see that You did not punish me or desert me. Instead, You *chose* me. You chose me to love these two boys more than I ever could have expected to love children. You chose me because they needed a special mom, an advocate, a mother with unconditional love. You chose me so that I could lend a voice, a hug, and encouragement to other parents of special needs' children. Thank you, Lord, for choosing me.

Furthermore, because we are united with Christ, we have received an inheritance from God for he chose us in advance, and he makes everything work out according to his plan. Ephesians 11:1 NLT

You didn't choose me. I chose you. I appointed you to go and produce lasting fruit, so that the Father will give you whatever you ask for, using my name. John 15:16 NLT

Father,

On my first Mother's Day as a mother, our pastor said that being a mother was God's highest calling. I remember how sweet that Mother's Day was because in previous years I had longed for a baby, but I couldn't have one. Mother's Day had always been the saddest day of the year for me and I always left church in tears.

Lord, when I think of my role as Your highest calling, it frightens me a bit. I know that being a mother is an awesome responsibility and while I felt prepared for it before I became a mother, I no longer do. My dreams and expectations about motherhood are so different from my reality. I didn't expect it to be this hard. I wasn't prepared for children with special needs. That had never been a part of my life, so I am constantly in "catch-up" mode, researching what to do to help them.

Lord, I don't know why You placed this particular calling of motherhood on my life in the way that You did, but I do know that everything You do is intentional. Lord, I know you are not going to leave me out here on my own to try to muddle through how I am supposed to be the right mom that You chose for these two boys.

God, please do all that You desire to do through my circumstances and trials because I know You mean them for good. Thank You, God, for putting these children and these challenges into my life as part of what You are doing in this world. Please, Lord, let me be worthy to fulfill Your plan.

Strength and dignity are her clothing, and she laughs at the time to come. She opens her mouth with wisdom, and the teaching of kindness is on her tongue. She looks well to the ways of her household and does not eat the bread of idleness. Her children rise up and call her blessed; her husband also, and he praises her. Proverbs 31:25-28 ESV

Dear God,

I confess my feelings of resentment, jealousy, and self-pity. I know these feelings are wrong and so I give them to You so You can help me to deal with them. God, I am often jealous of parents who have "normal" children. They do not understand how lucky they are. When they send their children to kindergarten, they expect them to sit quietly in their desks, read as directed, and write down their answers in a timely manner. Those parents don't have to worry about whether their children will be disruptive, kick their teachers, be mean to other children, learn to tie their shoes, write the alphabet legibly, learn to read, and make friends.

Some of these parents look upon me and my children with contempt. They have no clue what it is like to live in our world. Please free me from these feelings and help me to be thankful for my children who are a special blessing from You. Teach me, Lord, that I am adequate to parent these children that You have given to me and help me to remember that You are always with me and that what others think doesn't matter to You and it shouldn't matter to me.

Search me, O God, and know my heart; try me and know my anxious thoughts; and see if there be any hurtful way in me, and lead me in the everlasting way. Psalm 139:23-24 NASB

Dear God,

Today, You sent a big snowstorm which is something that we don't get very often. This was the first snow that my oldest son had ever seen. To say that he was thrilled, excited, and joyful at the chance to play in the snow would be wildly understating his happiness. He lay down in the snow, rolled around in it, and took big handfuls of the snow and pressed them to his face. He stuck out his tongue, savoring the taste of new snow on his tongue. He laughed and giggled and spun around. His delight in the snow could not have been more obvious. After rolling around in it to his heart's content, he got up and ran through the snow and twirled in it like he was dancing. I simply watched, fully enjoying the chance to see him just have fun for once, like any other child. We have a large yard and he ran and twirled and tumbled through the snow until I thought he would surely just drop from utter exhaustion.

God, I am thankful for one of the best afternoons I have ever spent with my son. Your beautiful creation and his enjoyment of it, allowed me to share in and savor his joy, and for one afternoon made me forget about the problems swirling in our lives. Thank You for giving us a wonderful day and marvelous memories to treasure.

Thank God for this gift too wonderful for words! 2 Corinthians 9:15 NLT

This is the day the Lord has made. We will rejoice and be glad in it. Psalm 118:24 NLT

Dear God,

I am so distraught. My son cannot behave at school and he is constantly being suspended. Some days I drop him off at school and he is already in trouble by the time I get to my office. I cannot keep my mind on work. I'm constantly praying for a good day for him, just something that will give me a glimmer of hope that everything will get better. It seems that my prayers are never answered. Instead, each day is worse than the day before it.

God, I know that You are answering my prayers, just not the way that I want You to answer them. Please teach me patience. Please, Lord, reveal Your plans to me and help me to keep believing that You are in control. Lord, I know that You can make something beautiful out of everything. Although this situation seems very ugly to me, I know that You see beauty in it. Lord, please let me see the beauty also.

We can make our own plans, but the Lord gives the right answer. Proverbs 16:1 NLT

I am praying to you because I know you will answer, O God. Bend down and listen as I pray. Psalm 17:6 NLT

Why am I discouraged? Why is my heart so sad? I will put my hope in God! I will praise him again—my Savior and my God. Psalm 43:5 NLT

And we know that God causes everything to work together for the good of those who love God and are called according to his purposes for them. Romans 8:28 NLT

Dear God,

Today, we went to behavior therapy with our son. I cried as we sat in the waiting room before the behavioral therapy session began. When is this nightmare going to end? I just wanted my child to be "normal," but he wasn't and never would be. As I sat there, a lady who was also waiting with what appeared to be her grandson, came over and sat down next to me and put her arms around me. She spoke softly, reassuring me that everything was going to be all right. She encouraged me to pray for strength and then she just sat there, holding my hand, feeling my pain. No words were necessary. For that moment, we were just two mothers, bound by a similar experience, grieving the same type of situation, only she was obviously a lot more at peace and much further along in the process than me.

God, I am so thankful that You place godly people in my path when I need them the most. They remind me to rely on You and not on my own strength.

Two people are better off than one, for they can help each other succeed. If one person falls, the other can reach out and help. But someone who falls alone is in real trouble. Ecclesiastes 4:9-10 NLT

The heartfelt counsel of a friend is as sweet as perfume and incense. Proverbs 27:9 NLT

Dear God,

I love this Christian school where we placed our son in kindergarten. He has been in so much trouble here and I know that before long, we will have to remove him from the school. Lord, I am so thankful for the principal. She told me that every morning, she goes into his classroom and sits in his little chair and prays for him to have a good day. Lord, I am so touched by her love for him. If he can't survive in a school where someone prays for him every day, how will he ever make it through another school? Lord, please make the path clear to me and please provide the people who will be able to manage and educate my son.

I urge you, first of all, to pray for all people. Ask God to help them; intercede on their behalf and give thanks for them. 1 Timothy 2:1 NLT

Show me the right path, O Lord; point out the road for me to follow. Psalm 25:4 NLT

Dear God,

In an effort to find peace about this school situation with my son, I sat down this afternoon with my Bible and a stack of index cards and started looking up all the scriptures I could find on anxiety. I was in the middle of writing down, "Be anxious for nothing, but in everything. . ." when the phone rang. It was the principal and she said, "We have to talk." I silently tucked the index cards into my Bible and drove to the school, crying and praying all of the way. Lord, I don't know how to find peace in the midst of this storm, but I know that You want to give me peace. I pray that peace comes soon.

Do not be anxious about anything, but in every situation, by prayer and petition, with thanksgiving, present your requests to God. And the peace of God, which transcends all understanding, will guard your hearts and minds in Jesus Christ. Philippians 4: 6-7.

Now may the Lord of peace himself give you his peace at all times and in every situation. The Lord be with you all. 2 Thessalonians 3:16 NLT

Give all your worries and cares to God, for he cares about you. 1 Peter 5:7 NLT

Dear God,

I need strength, Lord, because my faith is crumbling. I know that bad news lies ahead and I don't feel able to deal with it appropriately. The continual battles with the school system have left me weak and feeling powerless. I know that my son is intelligent, but no one can see it because his behavior is so awful. Any progress that he makes one day is extinguished the next day.

Lord, I need strength to fight for my son and to be his advocate. I pray that You would lift this heavy cloud of sadness from me that prevents me from clearly seeing Your plan and implementing it. Please uplift my spirit and give me the perseverance to press forward so that my son can receive an appropriate education. I know that You have a perfect school for him somewhere. I pray that You would lead me to it.

"Keep on asking, and you will receive what you ask for. Keep on seeking, and you will find. Keep on knocking, and the door will be opened to you. For everyone who asks, receives. Everyone who seeks, finds. And to everyone who knocks, the door will be opened." Matthew 7:7-8 NLT

Let us hold tightly without wavering to the hope we affirm, for God can be trusted to keep his promises. Hebrews 10:23 NLT

Dear Lord,

Please restore my confidence in You. I am going through a tough period of discouragement and self-doubt. I am struggling with inadequacy and disappointment. So many things have gone wrong in the last few weeks and instead of turning to You, I have instead just wallowed in self-pity. At times like these, I have trouble believing that You have a purpose in the midst of all the chaos that surrounds me.

I am hurting because my children are hurting and my husband is hurting. Our family is coming apart at the seams. We are so divided over the problems in our home. The boys' aggression is taking a toll on our physical house in terms of damage, but also on our home, our family itself. We cannot enjoy family time. All our time at home is spent trying to keep people or things from being hurt. It breaks my heart to see the anguish in my children because of the pain caused by their minds and bodies that they cannot control.

Sometimes I feel like we're a big jigsaw puzzle, but no one can put us together. The pieces won't fit or maybe some are just missing. In any event, our lives are a jumbled mess. I spend all my time trying to soothe, comfort, fix and repair. Lord, I am broken. I need You to restore my soul and for You to remind me that You are here and that this season of my life is all part of Your plan. Lord, please wrap me in Your arms and restore me, Lord, so that I can be the wife and mother You want me to be.

*O God, listen to my cry! Hear my prayer! From the ends of the earth, I cry
to you for help when my heart is overwhelmed. Lead me to the towering
rock of safety. Psalm 61:1-3 NLT*

*Rejoice in our confident hope. Be patient in trouble, and keep on praying.
Romans 12:12 NLT*

Dear God,

Today we took our son to visit the new kindergarten that he will be attending. There were about six children, all with special needs. As my husband and I talked to the principal and teacher, our son surveyed the room and immediately decided to join in with the art project the other students were doing.

The teacher was great and she handled all the children with confidence, even while trying to answer our questions. She was calm and the children seemed happy. I knew, God, that You had provided a teacher that I could trust to help my son. Thank You so much for Your provision, Lord.

God, after we talked with the teacher, our son came over and tapped her on the side. She leaned down to talk to him. He asked her quietly, "Is this a class for kids with problems like me?" Lord, this question brought tears to my eyes because it was the first time I had ever heard him acknowledge that there was something different about him. The teacher looked at him with compassion and said, "Yes, this a classroom for kids just like you!"

Lord, I am so thankful that You provided this school, this class, and especially this teacher. I know the situation won't be perfect, but You are showing me that You do have a plan and that I need to allow You to make the correct provisions.

"For I know the plans I have for you," says the Lord. "They are plans for good and not disaster, to give you a future and a hope." Jeremiah 29:11 NLT

Dear God,

I am really struggling with the education situation for my son. I am thankful that he finally has a stable school situation, but I cannot come to terms with the fact that my son is in special education. Lord, this is not what I planned. I don't want him to be in a special needs' classroom. I want him to have a "normal" childhood. I want him to have the educational opportunities that I had. I cannot rid myself of the feeling that he has been "cheated." Why does he have to live in this nightmare?

I sat in his classroom today and I observed the other children. Most of them had much more severe disability issues than my son. Lord, am I supposed to be thankful that he only has Asperger's Syndrome? God, what is wrong with me that I cannot simply be thankful that he has a place to belong? Lord, I have to learn that this situation is not about me or my feelings. You created my son the way You did for a reason. I keep saying that I trust You, yet I still find myself hard at work trying to implement my own plans. Please help my faith in You to be strong. Help me to quit doubting that You are in control. I pray for peace, Lord.

Let us hold tightly without wavering to the hope we affirm for God can be trusted to keep his promise. Hebrews 10:23 NLT

So be strong and courageous! Do not be afraid and do not panic before them. For the Lord your God will personally go ahead of you. He will neither fail you nor abandon you. Deuteronomy 31:6 NLT

Dear God,

I am so thankful that today a teacher took the time to tell me something good about my son. I confess that I have become conditioned to hearing only negative remarks about him and his behavior. I know that he is difficult and challenging in the classroom. I just steel myself when an adult wants to speak to me about my son.

However, this teacher told me: "I've witnessed him initiate random acts of kindness. He has interacted politely at times and used excellent manners when addressing others. Please know that the lessons he's been taught at home, so far in his upbringing, he has listened to and learned. He is capable of more appropriate behavior than has been his norm."

Lord, thank You for these kind words from a teacher. I am especially thankful to hear that even though his brain and body are in constant turmoil, he has actually learned and put into action some things we tried to teach him. Thank you, Lord, for Your goodness.

Kind words are like honey—sweet to the soul and healthy for the body.
Proverbs 16:24 NLT

God,

I need to learn to be content in every situation. This is not easy to do. When good things happen, I am happy. When things go wrong, I am sad and sometimes even angry. I need to be satisfied in both situations, accepting them as Your will. Help me to accept difficult circumstances and let me recognize Your strength as You bring me through each one.

God, it has really been a struggle getting my oldest son settled in school. We went through three kindergartens before we found one that would work for him. I thank You so much for the provision of a one-to-one aide for my son. Thankfully, she is not scared of my son and she is firm, but fair with him. He has finally been able to start participating in class without being disruptive. He has begun to interact and play with other children in an appropriate manner. He has even patiently waited for his turn to play an educational game on the computer in his class.

Lord, I know that every day will not be perfect. Simply because he has one good day does not mean that the next one will be good. However, Father, I am able to see progress and that is so meaningful to me. I know that every good gift comes from You and I thank You so much for Your provision.

Thank You for hearing me when I call out to You. You hear every whisper, every prayer, every cry for help. You hear me when I cannot even find the words to say. You understand my tears and I know that You never leave me alone. People will fail me, but You never will. You are always there, holding me, understanding me, and loving me. Thank You for always responding to my call.

Not that I speak from want, for I have learned to be content in whatever circumstances I am. Philippians 4:11 NASB

You can be sure of this: The Lord set apart the godly for himself. The Lord will answer when I call to him. Psalm 4:3 NLT

Dear God,

I wonder sometimes if parents who have lost a child feel the way I do. Are there days when they somehow summon up the courage to sit and watch an endless stream of videos of their child alive and well, playing, laughing, smiling, kicking a soccer ball, blowing out candles on a birthday cake? Do they watch the lively little figure on the screen, all the while filled with disbelief that the life is gone and the dreams they dreamed for their child have shattered and disappeared? Or does watching the life on the screen somehow dull the ache they feel inside?

Lord, this has been one of the hardest lessons I have tried to learn through this experience. Like most parents, I had plans and dreams for my sons. Perhaps because we adopted them, and I knew what their lives would have been like otherwise, my dreams for them were very grand. It has taken this experience for me to learn that my plans for them and their futures are not the same as Your plans for them. I know this doesn't mean that my plans were bad. It just means that they weren't Your plans. God, please teach me to let go of my hopes and dreams for these children and to trust You with Your plan for their lives. Please use them, Lord, in ways that I cannot even imagine.

Now all glory to God, who is able, through his mighty power at work within us, to accomplish infinitely more than we might ask or think. Ephesians 3:20 NLT

Father,

I pray for safety for my family and myself. Life is very scary right now in our home. My son is filled with rage that manifests itself through yelling, kicking, hitting, biting, and throwing objects. It hurts me to see him in such turmoil and so filled with anger. I cannot begin to understand what he is feeling inside and why his autism makes him lash out at his family. I fear for our safety and for his. I pray that You would be our refuge and keep our family safe within Your arms.

Lord, this situation makes me feel so vulnerable. I don't want to be helpless. I feel that I should be able to do more to help my son. Teach me to lean on You, to look to You for patience, and to stop focusing on the future. Lord, help me to start living my life for this day, for today, and for each new day. I want to listen to Your voice and I desire Your wisdom. I want to carefully follow the direction that Your Holy Spirit is leading me.

Keep me safe, O God, for I have come to you for refuge. Psalm 16:1 NLT

God is our refuge and strength, always ready to help in times of trouble. Psalm 46:1 NLT

I wait quietly before God, for my victory comes from him. He alone is my rock and my salvation, my fortress where I will never be shaken. Let all that I am wait quietly before God, for my hope is in him Psalm 62:1-2, 5 NLT

Dear Lord,

Today I took my son to the doctor. We discussed his sensory issues, his dependence on rituals and routines to get him through the day, his inability to transition from one activity to another, and his motor skills and behavior issues. I told the doctor that I wouldn't want to be him, even for one minute. "He doesn't want to be him, either," the doctor said. Her comment silenced me. I had never thought about this situation from his point of view.

God, please give me a new perspective and remind me that this is not about me. Lord, please show me how to love him and give me strength and wisdom to be a good mother to him.

Trust in the Lord with all of your heart; do not depend on your own understanding. Proverbs 3:5

Dear Father,

Max Lucado calls them our "giants" and says we need to face them. We all know who or what our "Goliath" is. We recognize his thunderous walk and the sound of his booming voice. We all have giants who need to be slain with one smooth stone. David depended upon You to help him kill his giant. Father, I believe that You, the same God who helped David, will help me defeat my giant, too.

Lord, we have a giant that lives in our home and he commands too much time and respect. It is a giant so powerful and important that we have named it—"Autism" and we spell it with a capital "A." Autism terrorizes our family within our own four walls. Despite my best efforts, God, I have never dealt it more than a glancing blow that temporarily dazes it. Not once have I come even close to delivering a fatal stone to its forehead. In fact, unlike Goliath, the giant, Autism, refuses to fall with a single stone delivered by a determined mother. However, Father, I trust in You daily to empower me to take aim at the menacing giant with my slingshot and bring it forcibly and finally to its knees. Alone, I can do nothing, but with Your strength alone, I can conquer the giant.

For I can do everything through Christ, who gives me strength. Philippians 4:13 NLT

"Yes, I am the vine; you are the branches. Those who remain in me, and I in them, will produce much fruit. For apart from me you can do nothing." John 15:5 NLT

God,

My faith is being stretched to its limit. I don't know how to cope with this situation with my son. He is supposed to take medication, but he refuses. He can't swallow pills, so it makes it so much more difficult to get the medication in him. I've tried opening the capsules and sprinkling the contents on his food, but now he looks at the food before he eats it and refuses to eat "sprinkles." I've put the tablets in marshmallows and peanut butter and jelly sandwiches. Nothing works.

There is so much stress in our home that I fear it will explode. I want You to do something, Lord, but I don't even know what the something is. Without You, I cannot handle what life has dealt me. Please, help my faith to grow. A part of me just wants to give up, but I know that You can change my reaction to this situation. Please give me the strength to carry on and to make the right decisions because my children need me to be strong.

For you know that when your faith is tested, your endurance has a chance to grow. James 1:3 NLT

Dear God,

Today my oldest son said that he doesn't want to have autism. He just wants to be "normal." My heart breaks when I hear him say these words. God, I know that You made him and that You don't make mistakes. I can't begin to understand why You created him with autism, but You had a reason for doing so. The Bible says that You knitted him together in his mother's womb. You knew everything about his life before he was even born. Please help me to explain this to him so that he can understand it.

God, I want him to understand that when we go through troubled times, it is because You are shaping us into who You want us to be. You are a sculptor, carefully chipping away at us so that we can begin to resemble the image of us that You had in mind when You created us.

For you created my inmost being; you knit me together in my mother's womb. I praise you because I am fearfully and wonderfully made; your works are wonderful, I know that full well. Psalm 139:13-14 NIV

And yet, O Lord, you are our Father. We are the clay, and you are the potter. We all are formed by your hand. Isaiah 64:8 NLT

"I knew you before I formed you in your mother's womb. Before you were born I set you apart and appointed you as my prophet to the nations. Jeremiah 1:5 NLT

As you do not know the path of the wind or how the body is formed in a mother's womb, so you cannot understand the work of God, the maker of all things. Ecclesiastes 11:5 NIV

Dear Lord,

Today we got confirmation from their doctor that both boys have high-functioning autism. I am trying to view this information with an opened mind. In some ways, it surely won't be as hard, knowing what to expect. On the other hand, it scares me to have this kind of responsibility as a mother.

I ask for Your guidance, Lord. I know the path before me is not going to be easy. In some ways, I have barely been able to cope with one child with autism and now I have two. Lord, You created this family in Your wisdom. You knew when we adopted the boys exactly what our futures held. I am trusting in You to give our family strength, to surround us with friends and family that can guide us, and to hold our fragile family together.

Lord, I know what we have already been through and it has been really difficult. I often have trouble surrendering this situation to You. God, I come to You now, very troubled. My mind wants to cry out, "Really, God? Have I not been through enough?" However, my soul seeks Your comfort, Your wisdom, and Your grace.

The pastor has often said that "if God brings it to you, He will bring you through it." Lord, I am trusting right now in this truth. You have given me a situation that I cannot handle and I ask Your help, Lord, in bringing our family through these circumstances for Your glory. I am scared, Lord. Please give me courage.

For no one is cast off by the Lord forever. Though he brings grief, he will show compassion, so great is his unfailing love. For he does not willingly bring affliction or grief to anyone. Lamentations 3:31-33 NIV

"This is my command—be strong and courageous! Do not be afraid or discouraged. For the Lord your God is with you wherever you go." Joshua 1:9 NLT

Dear God,

I've never had a time in my life that You have seemed so distant from me. I have pleaded for You to help my sons and our family. However, nothing improves; it only gets worse. Lord, when I ask for Your help, I hear only silence in response. God, I know that You care about us, but I don't understand why You are not helping us.

As I pray, I feel foolish. "Helping us" is my way of saying that You should do what would make my life more comfortable. I view this situation only in my human experience. While I know deep down that You care very much for my family and me, it is so easy for me to feel discouraged.

Friends from church want to help and they have encouraged me to pray and to trust in You. I am adamant, "I *have* prayed. That's all I do. I have prayed more than I have ever prayed in my life, yet God is not doing anything." Lord, please forgive my unbelief. I know that You do hear my prayers and that You are doing something, even if I can't see what it is. Lord, I want to believe. Please help me to totally trust in You.

Let us not become weary in doing good, for at the proper time we will reap a harvest if we don't give up. Galatians 6:9 NIV

Dear God,

It is so hard for me to go to church. My emotions are so high and out of control. No matter how hard I try to pull myself together, there is always a song during worship that reduces me to tears. Today it was "Still." Lord, the words of that song give me hope. "Hide me now/Under Your Wings/ Cover me/ Within Your mighty hand/When the oceans rise and thunders roar/I will soar with You above the storm/Father, You are King over the flood/I will be still/Know You are God." Lord, I sing the words, but I want to do more than sing, I want to know and believe that You are in control.

Lord, the imagery of that song mirrors my life which has become a constant storm. As a human, I cannot grasp that You have both planned and willed autism into my life. I want to learn to be still and know that You have a plan and that You are in control. I seek shelter under Your wings.

Have mercy on me, my God, have mercy on me, for in you I take refuge. I will take refuge in the shadow of your wings until the disaster has passed. Psalm 57:1 NIV

He will cover you with his feathers. He will shelter you with his wings. His faithful promises are your armor and protection. Psalm 91:4 NLT

Dear God,

I am so thankful that you have given us good friends at church. One couple always saves us a seat. They know we are having difficulties with our sons, but they don't know the extent of what we face. However, when I get overcome with emotion during the worship songs, she simply reaches over and puts her arm around me or squeezes my hand. Lord, these simple gestures mean so much to me. It shows that people care, even when they don't know or can't understand the depth of my pain. God, I don't always need someone to talk to me or ask me questions, I just need to know that someone is there for me. Thank you, Lord, for placing wonderful people like this in my life.

Two people are better off than one, for they can help each other succeed. If one person falls, the other can reach out and help. But someone who falls alone is in real trouble. Likewise, two people lying close together can keep each other warm. But how can one be warm alone? A person standing alone can be attacked and defeated, but two can stand back-to-back and conquer. Three are even better, for a triple-braided cord is not easily broken. Ecclesiastes 4:9-12 NLT

Dear God,

My oldest son has been saying strange things to me for the last several days. Tonight he said, "Don't cry when I die, Mommy." Of course, that made me cry. Lord, it seems that all I do lately is cry. Tears are always streaming down my face. God, what is happening to my little boy? Why don't You do something to help him? Lord, I know I shouted this question at You and I am sorry. Lately, it seems that I can't talk to You without shouting. I guess I think that You are not hearing me. However, deep down, I know that You are hearing me, but I am not listening to what You have to say. Please open my heart to be receptive to Your voice.

How miserable I am! I feel like a fruit picker after the harvest who can find nothing to eat. Not a cluster of grapes or a single early fig can be found to satisfy my hunger. Micah 7:1 NLT

As for me, I look to the Lord for help. I wait confidently for God to save me, and my God will certainly hear me. Micah 7:7 NLT

Dear Lord,

I talked to my pastor today and poured out all the problems about my oldest son. I asked him why You would make a child with autism, why You would allow a little child to suffer, why You chose our family? Lord, he told me something that I already knew deep down. You do not always make Your purposes clear to us while we are on this Earth.

God, that is a hard fact to live with because my human nature demands answers. Please show me that You are in control and help me to accept that You have a purpose for this trial and that You will reveal it to me one day. Lord, I know that You must have an awesome plan because You are an awesome God.

Many are the plans in the mind of a man, but it is the purpose of the Lord that will stand. Proverbs 19:21 ESV

For my thoughts are not your thoughts, neither are your ways my ways, declares the Lord. For as the heavens are higher than the earth, so are my ways higher than your ways and my thoughts than your thoughts. Isaiah 55:8-9 ESV

The Lord will work out the plans for my life—for your faithful love, O Lord, endures forever. Don't abandon me, for you made me. Psalm 138:8 NLT

Dear God,

Another thing my pastor told me is that sometimes You give us situations in our lives so that You can use our experience to comfort others, just as You have comforted us. Lord, I am a long way from being able to provide comfort to anyone else. I can barely make it from day-to-day. However, I pray that one day I will be able to comfort others by sharing how You brought us through this experience. God, please use my circumstances in the glorious unfolding of Your story.

Lord, each day I get a little closer to realizing how You are using me and my family. Lord, I certainly don't have solutions to my own problems, but I thank You for using me to just listen and lend comfort to other mothers. God, I have nothing to offer them except a hug and understanding. It seems like so little, but God please use it for Your good.

All praise to God, the Father of our Lord Jesus Christ. God is our merciful Father and the source of all comfort. He comforts us in all our troubles so that we can comfort others. When they are troubled, we will be able to give them the same comfort God has given us. For the more we suffer for Christ, the more God will shower us with his comfort through Christ. 2 Corinthians 1: 3-5 NLT

Dear God,

It has been a really rough week with my sons. There has been trouble at school every day and problems in the neighborhood with other children. I feel so defeated. When life is the toughest, I find myself running from You instead of running toward You. Why is it that I just want to hide when life becomes unbearable? Why isn't that the time that I seek You more?

I already know that I cannot handle things on my own, yet I hide myself away from You. Lord, I know that hiding will not solve my problems and that only You can restore peace in my life. I am thankful that You reach out to me, even when I try to hide from You. Please help me to seek You and Your wisdom and to know that with You in my life, I can overcome all the problems I face. Please help me to run into Your everlasting arms for I know that there is safety in Your arms. God, when I run into Your protective arms, I will not be defeated. I will be victorious. Your everlasting arms are never exhausted.

I've already run for dear life, straight to the arms of God. So why would I run away now? Psalm 11:1-2 The Message

The eternal God is your refuge, and his everlasting arms are under you. Deuteronomy 33:27a NLT

Dear God,

It's Christmas time and I'm decorating the tree. I've hung the store-bought ornaments and now I grab the two bags of homemade ornaments featuring my children's pictures. Some of them were made by the boys in daycare and preschool and some I made from their elementary school pictures. I take out the first few ornaments that have pictures of the boys as babies and I marvel at how tiny they were. I trace their little faces with my finger. Next, I start hanging the toddler ornaments. I look at the happy, innocent faces as I remember the days before autism became a household word in our family. I think about the dreams, hopes, and desires we had for those little boys—back when we believed they could become anything they wanted to be. If only they could have stayed little like that. A tear falls on the construction paper backing of one of the ornaments.

God, I can't do this. It hurts too much to remember. I didn't do a good job being their mother. I wish I could do it all over again and get it right this time. A cascade of tears follows and then calmness sets in. I feel Your holy presence as You gently tell me, "You did exactly what I asked of you. I made these boys especially for you because I wanted you to be their mother. I planned their lives and yours. I will always be with you and with them."

Many are the plans in the mind of a man, but it is the purpose of the Lord that will stand. Proverbs 19:21 ESV

Dear God,

Our family has been through a lot of adversity, but You are always there to bring us through. I know that there will be more troubles ahead, but You already know what they are going to be. You have a plan. It is not my plan and Your Word says that Your plan is for my welfare and not for calamity. I must trust in You to execute Your plan, knowing that it is for my good.

Lord, I am thankful that You do not let me glimpse into the future to see how things will work out. My human nature wants to know the answers right now, but God, You reveal them to me in Your own time. You unfold Your plan before me in tiny pieces because I am not able to comprehend the depth of all that You have envisioned for my sons and me.

God, You know what each day will bring, every high and low, every twist and every turn. I must leave each day in Your hands, for only You know what is best for me. Each day is a gift from You and I know You lead me, even when I cannot feel Your Presence.

For I know the plans I have for you," declares the Lord, "plans to prosper you and not to harm you, plans to give you hope and a future." Jeremiah 29:11 NLT

The Lord our God has secrets known to no one. We are not accountable for them, but we and our children are accountable forever for all that he has revealed to us, so that we may obey all the terms of these instructions. Deuteronomy 29:29 NLT

O Lord,

I must learn to trust in You more. It's not my natural instinct to call upon You in the midst of chaos in our home. Teach me to let the times of tumult, like tonight, become opportunities for me to grow in my understanding of You.

God, I asked my son to take his books and papers to his room. He didn't want to go to his room because the lights were not on and he is afraid of the dark. I don't know why I didn't just go and turn on the lights, but I didn't. Instead, he got very agitated. He began kicking his dad, then he flipped over the bar stool his brother was sitting on and they both landed on the floor with a large thud. He ran around the kitchen, looking for anything to destroy or anyone to hurt.

Next, he picked up a green magic marker and scribbled on his hands and then rubbed the ink all over his face and hands. I tried to make him laugh by telling him how funny his face looked. Humor did not diffuse the situation, like it sometimes does. He continued to rub the green magic marker all over his face and body. He took off his shirt and made his chest and tummy green.

I knew the right way to handle this situation was to remain calm, but I didn't. I began yelling at him. I felt so small inside when I did this. I started walking back to his bathroom with him to wash his face and body. He didn't want to wash because he wants to look scary. God, he *did* look scary. I told him he couldn't go to school looking that way. I wet a washcloth and put soap on it, but he didn't want to be washed. He grabbed the washcloth and flung it directly into my face. That finally made me cry and then he stopped and wrapped his wet, green arms around my waist and said that he loved me. The storm passed, but I question whether I am up to the task of being his mother. You assured me that I am.

Lord, You are my Shepherd. You tend me as part of Your flock and You gather the small lambs and carry them in Your heart. Lord, I am so thankful to be your lamb and I know that You care for me.

He will feed his flock like a shepherd. He will carry the lambs in his arms, holding them close to his heart. He will gently lead the mother sheep with their young. Isaiah 40:11 NLT

Then Jesus said, "Come to me, all of you who are weary and carry heavy burdens, and I will give you rest. Take my yoke upon you. Let me teach you, because I am humble and gentle at heart, and you will find rest for your souls. For my yoke is easy to bear, and the burden I give you is light. Matthew 11:28-30 NLT

Dear Father,

I know that You want me to trust You and to be deeply dependent on You. If I succeed on my own, I tend to rely upon myself and feel it is unnecessary to rely and depend upon You. When I have problems and failures, I must call on You for help. I must come to You with an open mind and open heart. I cannot ask or expect You to bless my plans. You have the power, not me.

God, one of the hardest lessons I'm having to learn while parenting autistic children is to let go of my dreams for them. I know that doesn't mean that my dreams are bad or wrong. It's just that my plans for my sons' futures are not Your plans. I want to learn to let go of my hopes and dreams for these children and to trust You instead with Your plan for their lives. Lord, I believe in the future, You will show me those plans and how I fit in them also.

I want to depend upon You to show me the path to take, even when it seems to me that the path is wrong. I must remember that You know the outcome and that I don't. Things that happen in my life are never unexpected to You because You have planned each thing and I must trust You completely because Your plan is always better than mine.

The Lord hears his people when they call to him for help. He rescues them from all their troubles. The Lord is close to the brokenhearted; he rescues those whose spirits are crushed. The righteous person faces many troubles, but the Lord comes to the rescue each time. For the Lord protects the bones of the righteous; not one of them is broken! Psalm 34: 17-22 NLT

God,

You can do anything. I can't set low expectations. I've prayed for my children to be healed for ten years and yet, I don't have an answer to this prayer. Ten years seems like a long time to me, but it is nothing in Your time—mere seconds, perhaps.

God, You are doing many things that I don't even know about. You set in motion the answers to my prayers before I can even begin to see the results, perhaps even before I say my prayers. You are able to make all things work together for good for those who love You. I can't get discouraged because it seems that my prayers are not answered, for You are constantly at work. I do nothing but cause stress for myself when I try to make things happen on my own, instead of waiting for You, Lord, to work in Your time.

A thousand years in your sight are like a day that has just gone by, or like a watch in the night. Psalm 90:4 NIV

Now all glory to God, who is able, through his mighty power at work within us, to accomplish infinitely more than we might ask or think. Ephesians 3:20 NLT

But you must not forget this one thing, dear friends: A day is like a thousand years to the Lord, and a thousand years is like a day. Romans 3:8 NLT

But those who wait on the Lord shall renew their strength; they shall mount up with wings like eagles; they shall run and not be weary; they shall walk and not faint. Isaiah 40:31 NKJV

And we know that God causes all things to work together for good to those who love God, to those who are called according to His purpose. Romans 8:28 NASB

God,

You know everything about me. I can probably fool some people, but never You. You know my troubles and my cares, my hurts and my sorrows. You want me to share them with You and release them to You. Only then, can You take my weaknesses and transform them into strengths.

God, I confess that I have a problem with my son being in special education. My mind goes back to when I was in junior high school. There was a special education classroom right across the hall from my social studies class. I recall being curious about the students and peering into the room to catch a glimpse of them. I didn't make fun of them, but I remember being somewhat scared of them. I don't know what I thought would happen to me if I had some incidental contact with them, but I didn't want to find out either.

I feel so ashamed of those thoughts I had so many years ago. God, is that how people are going to feel about my son—like they don't want to get too close to him just in case? I have trouble accepting the fact that my son belongs in special education. Lord, please help me to accept this fact and to learn to be thankful that he has a place to belong where he is getting help with his problems. I want Your power to rest upon me. You alone can make me strong.

The Lord doesn't see things the way you see them. People judge by outward appearance, but the Lord looks at the heart. 1 Samuel 16:7b NLT

But he said to me, "My grace is sufficient for you, for my power is made perfect in weakness." Therefore, I will boast all the more gladly about my weaknesses, so that Christ's power may rest on me. That is why, for Christ's sake, I delight in weaknesses, in insults, in hardships, in persecutions, in difficulties. For when I am weak, then I am strong. 2 Corinthians 12:9-10 NIV

God,

We have highs and lows in the lives You have planned for us. Even though we dislike the troubles and trials of our lives, they are necessary, and we must endure them. They are all part of Your glorious plan for us. I know this, Lord, yet I struggle through the troubles. It hurts me when I see my children hurting. I want to take all their pain away, so they don't have to endure it. I am impatient for You to reveal to me why their pain and hurt are necessary.

I know that there are no shortcuts on the road to heaven. We must trust You when things go wrong, according to our standard of "wrong." This is our standard of measurement, but not Yours. Please help me, Lord, to fix my gaze on You and be content that You have a perfect plan in place for my life and the lives of my sons.

For our present troubles are small and won't last very long. Yet they produce for us a glory that vastly outweighs them and will last forever. So don't look at the troubles we can see now; rather, we fix our gaze on things that cannot be seen. For the things we see now will soon be gone, but the things we cannot see will last forever. 2 Corinthians 4:17-18 NLT

Dear God,

I know You want me to be wholly dependent on You. You want me to bring all my cares, my hurts, my disappointments, and my troubles to You. When I am afraid about what will happen with my sons, You are there to calm my fears. Lord, I am afraid that other children will take advantage of my children. I have seen it happen and it breaks my heart. One day when my oldest son was selling candy bars for school, he came home from after school care with only a few dollars and hardly any candy bars. Some of the older children took candy bars from him and said they would pay later and other kids asked to "borrow" some of his candy money.

My children are so trusting of others and they want to have friends. It is hard for them to discern the difference between real friendship and other children using them. I need to be more aware and watchful for situations where older children try to convince my sons to do things they shouldn't do or blame them for things they didn't do. God, please watch over my sons and keep them safe from others who would harm them.

Thank You for wrapping Your arms securely around my family to protect us from all harm. You are always there to catch us when we fall. Your arms are everlasting and Your grip on us never loosens. Thank You, Lord, for sheltering us beneath Your wings, for rescuing this struggling mother and for protecting my family and me. You are a great God and greatly to be praised.

This I declare about the Lord: He alone is my refuge, my place of safety; he is my God, and I trust him. For he will rescue you from every trap and protect you from deadly disease. He will cover you with his feathers. He will shelter you with his wings. His faithful promises are your armor and protection. Do not be afraid of the terrors of night, nor the arrow that flies in the day. Psalm 91:2-5 NLT

The eternal God is your refuge, and his everlasting arms are under you. Deuteronomy 33:27a NLT

Dear God,

Worry and anxiety have a way of overtaking me when my days are filled with problems with the boys. Their outbursts and anger are scary to them and to me. I feel so helpless when they have meltdowns. Often, I have no idea what has caused them to meltdown and I don't think that they know either. I want to be able to stop their anguish and destroy whatever it is that makes them feel so angry. Lord, I know that when they are lashing out, it is their way of communicating. I know other people don't understand it as a form of communication, and I often do not understand what they are trying to tell me through their agony, but You know, Lord.

I must trust in You, O God. Help me to discern and follow Your will, not mine. Show me the path to take that You have already provided that will lead to the best for my sons and our family. Teach me to see the hidden blessings that You have for us. Help me to accept things in my life the way that they are, knowing that You already have a purpose in mind to turn, what seem to me to be trials, into triumphs.

Trust in the Lord with all your heart; do not depend on your own understanding. Seek his will in all you do and he will show you which path to take. Proverbs 3:5-6 NLT

God,

You are an ever-present help in times of trouble. Please give me the faith to trust in You and to allow You to guide and control my day. Teach me to hand my problems and worries over to You each day so that I can receive and bask in Your peace. I know that I will never run out of things to worry about, so help me to make the choice each day to choose not to worry and to allow You to control my life, which You, in Your wisdom, have planned. Help me to see my problems in Your light and teach me to be joyful even during rough times.

I know that You long to help me when my days are filled with difficulties with my children. I confess that there are days that I want to just throw up my hands and quit. I've said countless times, "I can't do this anymore!" However, You are always there when I reach this point. Regardless of how exhausted or inadequate I feel, You always reassure me that I can keep on and that You are there to help me each step of the way. Thank You for Your faithfulness.

God is our refuge and our strength, a very present help in trouble. Therefore, we will not fear, though the earth should change and though the mountains slip into the heart of the sea. Psalm 46:2 NASB

Nevertheless, I am continually with you; you have taken hold of my right hand. Psalm 73:23 NASB

You will keep in perfect peace all who trust in you, all whose thoughts are fixed on you. Isaiah 26:3 NLT

Dear Heavenly Father,

This afternoon I was watching a documentary on television about autism. I was trying to keep my oldest son from knowing what I was doing because ever since he learned he has autism, he gets very upset when he hears the word. He generally shouts at me, "I want to be NORMAL!!" Lord, I want him to be "normal" too.

I constantly tell him: "God made you just the way He wanted you to be. I don't know the reason why He gave you autism, but I can tell you that God does not make mistakes. He wants to use you to change other lives and to help other families. God chose you to be my son, so we have to trust God to show us the way."

The documentary was almost over when he found me. Instead of being angry, he sat down and watched the rest of the program with me which dealt with the importance of early intervention. When it was over, he looked at me and asked, "Mommy, why didn't you get me early treatment? It might have helped me." Lord, the tears spilled down my cheeks as I told him that I just didn't know soon enough about his diagnosis to get early intervention. God, I know he will never understand the depth of my sorrow about the lost opportunity to get him early treatment. Lord, one day, please have my son to forgive me and please help me to forgive myself also.

. . . Who are you, a mere human being to argue with God? Should the thing that was created say to the one who created it, "Why have you made me like this?" Romans 9:20 NLT

God,

I know you want me to spend time with You every day. You don't want the "leftover" time I have, if any. I don't want to let dealing with autism and its many problems to keep me from seeking You. I know You should be my first priority. You want to be first and not shoved to the back in case I have a few minutes left at the end of the day. I know that if I trust in You and spend time with You each day, You will bless my life and ease my struggles. To accomplish this, I have to relinquish control of my life, my children, and my time to You.

Lord, I confess that it is hard for me to turn my mind "off" to the continual problems with my children. When I try to pray, I always have one ear opened to listen for problems. Please teach me how to release these problems to You, so that I can give You all of me. I know that when I give You all of me, You will guide and comfort me.

Thank you, God, that You are always with me, both in the good times and the bad. You hold onto me and never let go. I can feel that I am hitting rock-bottom, yet You stretch out Your gentle hand and hold me safely in Your arms. Thank you, God, for never letting me down and for never letting me fall.

Do not fear; for I am with you; do not anxiously look about you, for I am your God. I will strengthen you, surely I will help you, surely I will uphold you with my righteous right hand. Isaiah 41:10

For I am the Lord your God, who upholds your right hand, who says to you, "Do not fear, I will help you." Isaiah 41:13

48

God,

Please help me to use my problems with my children to learn what You are trying to teach me. Everything in my life happens because it is part of the master plan that You designed for me. That includes autism and all it is doing to my family. To learn from my problems, I must trust You completely and as strange as it sounds, learn to be thankful for my problems. For it is when I face troubles and trials that You are trying to teach me the most. Help me to live above the circumstances of my crazy and cluttered life. Let Your peace flourish in my life, especially during times of trouble.

God, sometimes when I look at the oil painting of my life up close, it seems very ugly. It looks like angry dabs of paint thrown upon the canvas in no particular pattern. But when You prompt me to stand back and view the painting from a distance, from Your perspective, I can see the beautiful canvas You have created. Thank you for being the Master Creator and Designer of my life.

I have told you all this so that you may have peace in me. Here on earth you will have many trials and sorrows. But take heart, because I have overcome the world. John 16:33 NLT

And yet, O Lord, you are our Father. We are the clay, and you are the potter. We are all formed by your hand. Isaiah 64:8 NLT

For we are God's masterpiece. He has created us anew in Christ Jesus, so we can do the good things he planned us for long ago. Ephesians 2:10 NLT

O God,

It is so comforting to know that You are always with me. When I am joyous, You are there and when I face difficult times, You are there. I am never alone. You continually hold onto me. Even though, I lose my way sometimes, You are still there, holding onto me and lifting me up. You keep me completely secure and safe in Your hands. Thank You for never letting go of me.

God, I am so thankful that You provide moments for me to rejoice in Your goodness. I was so concerned about my son having to ride the bus to his new school. I've been astonished that riding the bus is the best part of his day. He loves everything about riding the bus. He flies to the end of the driveway when he hears the bus coming and he has a huge smile on his face when he boards the bus.

You provided a lovely aide for him on the bus. Her name is Mrs. Jewell, which is his grandma's name and he feels drawn to her. She sits right beside him on the bus, although there are dozens of empty seats. He hugs her every morning and she beams with pleasure when she sees him. Each afternoon, she asks about his day and shows a genuine interest in him.

God, I praise You for providing Mrs. Jewell for my son. It is so comforting to know that there are other people who adore my son and who are looking out for his best interests. It also eliminates a source of worry for me because

I know he won't have behavior problems on the bus. Thank You, Lord, for Your goodness.

The eternal God is your refuge, and his everlasting arms are under you. Deuteronomy 33:27a NLT

God,

It is so hard for me to learn to let go of the people I love. I know that I fight for control of them sometimes instead of releasing them to You. I specifically pray that You would help me to release my sons to You, so that You can work wonders and miracles in their lives. Lord, what I choose to hold onto, You cannot use, but when I open my hand to release what I am holding, You give me even more in return.

Lord, I ask for the strength and faith I need to release my sons into Your hands. Help me, Lord, not to live in fear of dangers that could befall them. Instead, let me live in peace, knowing that You are in control of every breath they breathe. Please deliver me from doubt and fear. Let me be as brave as the mother of Moses, who had the courage to place her son in a basket and send him down the Nile River. Give me the courage to place my sons into Your care where You will protect them from all manner of danger. Lord, You alone created and gave to me the precious gift of my two sons. I know that You are fully capable of keeping them safe in all ways because You are everywhere and everything is within Your control.

Help me to learn to live one day at a time as You have ordained. Let me release my children, my worries, and my anxieties into Your care and to believe that You have a time and purpose for everything.

To everything there is a season, a time for every purpose under heaven.
Ecclesiastes 3:1 NKJV

Rise during the night and cry out. Pour out your hearts like water to the
Lord. Lift up your hands to him in prayer, pleading for your children.
Lamentations 2:19a NLT

God,

When I am tired and everything is going wrong (which seems to be most of the time), teach me to say, "I trust You, Lord and I give this day to You." Help me to release every problem, every care and every concern to You and then allow me to rest in Your everlasting arms. Before my day even begins, You know each thing that I will confront—every trial or blessing. Help me to accept both the joy and the sorrow as part of Your great plan for my life.

I am so thankful that I don't have to have all the answers and that I can trust in You to guide me to make correct decisions. Lord, there are so many times that I want to rely on myself instead of turning to You. Sometimes that is because I want a quick resolution, instead of waiting on the plan You have set in motion. Lord, please strengthen my faith, so that I will trust and believe in You and not doubt.

Today, I trust in You, Lord, to guide and protect my children. You know everything that will happen in their lives today. Lord, I am so amazed at how much You care for them. Thank You for loving them and guiding them.

If any of you lacks wisdom, you should ask God, who gives generously to all without finding fault, and it will be given unto you. But when you ask, you must believe and not doubt, because the one who doubts is like a wave of the sea, blown and tossed by the wind. That person should not expect to receive anything from the Lord. James 1:5-7 NIV

What good is it, dear brothers and sisters, if you say you have faith but don't show it by your actions? Can that kind of faith save anyone? James 2:14 NLT

Trust in the Lord with all your heart and do not lean on your own understanding. In all your ways acknowledge Him, and He will make your paths straight. Do not be wise in your own eyes. Proverbs 3:5-7 NASB

God,

Please help me to rejoice in each day that You have made. Help me to live within the boundaries of each day, one hour at a time, so that worry and anxiety about tomorrow don't creep into my heart and steal my trust. I know that before one day has even ended, I am already dreading the problems I may face with my children tomorrow.

God, if You expected us to do everything today, You wouldn't have created tomorrow. Help me to keep that thought foremost in my heart and mind. Help me to trust You completely, even when things go wrong in our home or the boys have problems at school and in the neighborhood.

Please teach me to rejoice in each day and help me to find at least one small thing to be thankful for every day. I am always ready to call on You in times of trouble, but I fail to offer prayers of thanksgiving. Help me to be more mindful of Your blessings. Let me learn to be thankful in all circumstances. I am so thankful for my sons and my husband and all that You have fulfilled in my life through them.

This is the day the Lord has made. We will rejoice and be glad in it. Psalm 118:24 NLT

So do not worry about tomorrow, for tomorrow will take care of itself. Each day has enough trouble of its own. Matthew 6:34 NASB

Rejoice always, pray without ceasing; in everything give thanks; for this is God's will for you in Christ Jesus. 1 Thessalonians 4:16 NASB

God,

Thank you for designing me to need You and for making that need constant. Don't allow me to ever think that I can handle life on my own and that I don't need You. You give me everything I need for each day. You give me the strength and courage to be the mother that my sons need to guide them through life. You have blessed me with patience to deal with the everyday struggles that our family faces. However, sometimes, I feel discouraged and want to give up. I have said, "I can't do this anymore," more than once.

But, God, You are always here to guide me through the storms. You never leave me, even when I am trying to go it alone. Please help me to live each day without worrying about the next day or even further into the future. Set me free to let Your grace fill my life. You have a never-ending supply of love and peace, which You freely give to me. Thank You for Your love and grace.

Be strong and courageous. Do not be afraid or terrified because of them, for the Lord your God goes with you; he will never leave you nor forsake you. Deuteronomy 31:6 NIV

The Lord is near to all who call on him, to all who call on him in truth. Psalm 145:18 NIV

God,

Please teach me not to fear because You will bring good out of every situation I encounter in life. I am already experiencing personal growth and a closer walk with You because of my sons. When You allow trouble into my life, You equip me to handle it. I have been amazed at how I have been able to help my sons and advocate for them using skills I didn't even know I possessed. The simple truth is that You equip me. You give me strength, wisdom, and courage when I have none. Your Holy Spirit leads me when I don't know the way.

On my own, I can do nothing. I run from trouble instead of handing it to You. Lord, I am so thankful that You alone can make the impossible possible. God, I want my faith to grow so that I can confidently know that You can do anything!

For nothing will be impossible with God. Luke 4:37 NASB

Now all glory to God, who is able, through his mighty power at work within us, to accomplish infinitely more than we might ask or think. Ephesians 3:20 NLT

Dear God,

Find rest, my soul, in Christ alone. Lord, don't let my troubles and trials with my children cause me to take my eyes off You. I am uncertain what lies ahead for my family, but You know. In Your wisdom, You do not allow me to see into the future that You have planned. Instead, You call me to simply trust in You anew each day because You will fully equip me each day for whatever comes my way. If I could see into the future, I would be fearful and anxious. That is not what You want. You have an entire plan that I don't know or understand and You reveal it to me bit-by-bit, day-by-day and You guide me through each day.

Today is Your day that You have called into being. God, I am so thankful that You provide new mercies each day, that they are always enough, and never rationed. Please erase my anxious thoughts from my mind so that I remember that I face nothing alone. You are always with me. Give me strength to embrace each day unafraid. God, if You are with me, who can be against me?

The faithful love of the Lord never ends! His mercies never cease. Great is his faithfulness; his mercies began afresh each morning. Lamentations 3:22-23 NLT

What shall we say about such wonderful things as these? If God is for us, who can ever be against us? Romans 8:31 NLT

God,

I fear that my worry drowns out Your voice. My mind is so filled with thoughts, dread, and despair that I cannot hear You through the clutter. Today was a terrible day for my son at school. His behavior report indicated that he had "scribbled all over another student's paper when he didn't want to do the assignment; used watercolors, but when he didn't like his painting, he threw water all over the table; tried 'free play,' but he threw toys at other children and all over the classroom; worked well on the computer for a few minutes, but when something went wrong, he began slamming the computer keyboard on the table; tried to make him stop damaging the keyboard, so he turned his attention to kicking and hitting his aide; dug his nail into his aide's arm; jumped off tables; started jumping into the aide's body like it was fun; pushed and hit another child; and had difficulty transitioning from music to story time, so he began to kick another child." Lord, all of this happened today.

Please quiet my thoughts and fill my heart and mind with peace. Cast out my worries, for no amount of worrying will change anything at all. It certainly won't improve anything. God, help me to recognize my weakness and Your strength. Allow me to bask in Your peace.

And He said to me, "My grace is sufficient for you, for power is perfected in weakness. Most gladly, therefore, I will rather boast about my weaknesses, so that the power of Christ may dwell in me. Therefore, I am well content with weaknesses, with insults, with distresses, with persecutions, with difficulties, for Christ's sake; for when I am weak, then I am strong. 2 Corinthians 12:9-10 NASB

God,

I am so thankful that I am not alone. You are so close to me. I can feel You in my heart and my life. You are like air to me. You provide my breath to me. When I feel panic and despair because of problems with the boys, I long to reach out and touch Your gentleness and goodness. Your Holy Spirit speaks quietly to my mind and directs my path. Please direct my steps so that I can enjoy the day You have planned for me.

Lord, I cannot face this day alone because there is too much happening for me to handle it on my own. The school is going to move one of my sons to a different class at a new school. I know that he will not like the change. He doesn't do well with transitions and he won't understand why this change is happening. I am just so tired of fighting this particular principal to get her to do the right thing for him. I pray that You would allow something good to come from this move and that he will not fight it.

Thank you for allowing Your Holy Spirit to guide and comfort me as I face the new day that awaits me. Thank You for Your love and mercy that encourage and surround me each day. I could not make it without Your love and Your guiding hand.

So do not fear, for I am with you; do not be dismayed for I am your God. I will strengthen and help you; I will uphold you with my righteous right hand. Isaiah 41:10 NIV

The Lord himself goes before you and will be with you; he will never leave you nor forsake you. Do not be afaid; do not be discouraged. Deuteronomy 31:8 NIV

And be sure of this: I am with you always, even to the end of the age. Matthew 28:20b NLT

God,

Sometimes I cheat myself out of joy and happiness. I often want my life to be perfect and I want to delay happiness until I attain that goal. Realistically, I know that my life will never be perfect, not until I am with You in heaven. Help me to release my craving for perfection. Allow me to experience the joy and happiness that You have for me on this Earth.

Lord, on my own so many times, I have tried to plan the "perfect" birthday party or event for my sons and they didn't turn out as I expected. I set my standards way too high. I belittle myself if I am not perfect or I don't meet my own high expectations. Lord, I know You don't expect me to be perfect, because no one is except Jesus. I want to find the joy and happiness in the little things in life—the things that aren't perfect, yet they're good. My children don't expect perfection. Help me to enjoy the happiness that they find in the smallest of situations and stop fretting when things aren't the way I want them to be.

The Lord is my strength and shield. I trust him with all my heart. He helps me and my heart leaps with joy. I burst out in songs of Thanksgiving. Psalm 28:7 NLT

May the God of hope fill you with all joy and peace as you trust in him, so that you may overflow with hope by the power of the Holy Spirit. Romans 15:13 NLT

Lord,

Please help me to focus on the present. Don't let me waste time regretting the past or worrying about the future. Remind me that my future is in Your hands and solely within Your control. Help me to resist the temptation to "go it alone" and instead, guide me each step of the way. Free me from the fear deep inside me that threatens to steal my joy. Teach me to release all my worries and troubles to You.

People are always telling me that "God won't give you more than you can handle." But, Lord, life itself is more than I can handle. You don't want me to carry my heavy burdens. You want me to surrender them to You. That is what faith is all about. Everything is more than I can handle, but not more than You can handle.

I know that my biggest problem is worrying about the future. I worry about my children each day as they go to school. I worry about what will happen to them. Will they misbehave? Will they be in trouble? Will they be bullied or harassed? Will they be hurt? Will they be safe? Lord, please help me to release these worries to You and not to hold on to them. I want You to be in control, not me.

They do not fear bad news; they confidently trust the Lord to care for them. Psalm 112:7 NLT

But Lord, be merciful to us, for we have waited for you. Be our strong arm each day and our salvation in times of trouble. Isaiah 33:2 NLT

God,

I crave your peace, the inner peace that only You can give. I know it must hurt You when I fill my mind with worry and anxiety. Help me to give more than "lip service" to my longing for peace. Teach me to search for the hidden treasure of peace that You are yearning to give me. I want to replace my worry with Your peace. Please clear my mind of clutter and useless worries. Only Your peace can quell the anguish in my soul. Help me to quiet my soul and to recognize that You alone are God. Please help me to search for You with my whole heart.

God, when things are going well for me, I tend not to need You as much and I try to control my own life without Your help. That is why I need trials, Lord, so that You can draw me close to You. Thank You, God, for teaching me through my sons. I have learned so much from the problems we have encountered. There have been a lot of problems, but You are always there for me. God, I don't understand how people can go through situations like mine without You in their lives. Thank You for providing peace, guidance, and comfort to me.

I am counting on the Lord; yes, I am counting on him. I have put my hope in his word. I long for the Lord more than the sentries long for the dawn, yes, more than sentries long for the dawn. Psalm 130:5-6 NLT

And the peace of God, which surpasses all comprehension, will guard your hearts and your minds in Christ Jesus. Philippians 4:7 NASB

You will seek Me and find Me when you search for Me with all your heart. Jeremiah 29:15 NASB

Lord,

I have pain and sorrow in my life. I want to thank You from the depths of my heart for my circumstances, even though my mind tells me that it is alright for me to complain about my circumstances. God, You see me when I suffer because I suffer when my children do. It is so frustrating to have other people judge my parenting or the way my children behave. Sometimes, I wonder if other people had to live my life, would they be more understanding?

I know that I make mistakes in the way I parent my children, but I am trying my hardest to do everything right and to do it in a way that is pleasing to You. I know I'm not a "perfect" mother. I make mistakes. I have and will falter many times. I will have many days when I think I cannot do this any longer.

Help me to remember that You can bring about good from any situation. Draw me closer to You and wipe away my tears. Please allow my circumstances to cause me to seek You even more. Please give me wisdom to cry out in thankfulness to You.

Consider it all joy, my brethren, when you encounter various trials, knowing that the testing of your faith produces endurance. And let endurance have its perfect result, so that you may be perfect and complete, lacking in nothing. James 1:2-4 NASB

O God,

This day has been full of tears. I wanted to make my son's eighth birthday special, so I planned a bowling party for him. At first, everything went fine. Every time he knocked over some pins, he celebrated by jumping around, thrusting his hands in the air, doing a little dance, and shouting out that he knocked over pins. He also tried to "high-five" anyone who was nearby. It was delightful to watch him have such a wonderful time.

However, a woman who was bowling in the next lane came and asked if the children belonged to me. I told her yes and that it was a birthday party and I pointed out my sons. She said my son was bothering her and her friends when he did his little celebration dance. I apologized and told her that he was a little over-exuberant due to the party. I also explained that he had an autism disorder.

A few minutes later, the woman and her friends tapped me on the shoulder and she said, "That child is not autistic. I have babysat autistic children before and he is not autistic because he can talk." I suggested she mind her own business, but she didn't. She said, "Let me guess, all of the kids at this party are 'autistic' while making those little quote marks in the air. Then she added, "Have you ever heard of discipline?"

Lord, I lost it. I just wanted my child to have a happy birthday. I started crying. She went to get the manager and she complained to him about how the noise and the kids' behavior were ruining her evening. The manager told her, "that's how kids act. They can stay, but you need to leave!" The manager was so kind. He wouldn't even let me pay for the party.

My son saw my face was all red with tears streaming down it and he asked me, "Mom, is your face sad?" I just put my arms around him and told him I was fine. Another mom tried to comfort me, but how do you explain the ache that is so deep inside you when all you want is for your child to have fun like any "normal" child would do?

Thank You for allowing me to release my tears to You. God, I so look forward to the day when there will be no more tears, sadness, or pain. There will be no more situations that rob me of joy and peace. Anxiety and worry will no longer exist. I can hardly wait for the beauty of that day!

He will wipe every tear from their eyes, and there will be no more death or sorrow or crying or pain. All these things are gone forever. Revelation 21:4 NLT

Lord,

Thank You for creating this day. I know that it is not just a chance occurrence. Instead, You make and plan each day just for me. Help me to be adequately prepared for what awaits me each day. Otherwise, I won't be able to face the situations that will come. I want to rejoice in each day You have made.

God, You amaze me with the way you orchestrate situations and how You used my son over the weekend. He was selling candy bars for his school and we were going door-to-door in our neighborhood. I stood at the curb and let him go up to the front doors to make the sales. As we started walking down a new street, a police officer stopped us and asked if we had seen anyone suspicious in the neighborhood because someone's car had been stolen. We hadn't, so we continued with our business.

My son sprinted up to every house and made his little sales pitch and always came back with a fistful of dollars. At one house, he talked to the woman at the door for a few minutes and then called for me to come to the front door. When I did, I saw the woman was crying. It was her car that had been stolen. My son told her not to worry and that his Mom would pray for her and that God would fix everything. So, God, on her front door step, we prayed for peace and comfort for her. My son gave her a big hug and she, of course, bought some candy bars.

Today, when my husband came home from work, he said he had talked to a friend who lives in our neighborhood who had one of their cars stolen out of their driveway. I told him that we had gone to that house to sell candy bars right after the incident happened. My husband said his friend mentioned that a woman and little boy came by the house and prayed for his wife and that it made her feel much better. I told my husband, "that was us!" God, I knew that You planned for us to be there, selling candy bars at just the right time to comfort someone. Thank You for using my son in this special way.

This is the day that the Lord has made. We will rejoice and be glad in it. Psalm 118:24 NLT

The Lord says, "I will guide you along the best pathway for your life. I will advise you and watch over you." Psalm 32:8 NLT

O Lord, I will honor and praise your name for you are my God. You do such wonderful things! You planned them long ago, and now you have accomplished them. Isaiah 25:1 NLT

O God,

I don't know what lies ahead for my children, but You do. I am often fearful of the unknown, always expecting the worst possible thing to happen. You only allow me to see part of the picture, while You have the full view. Help me to trust You and to know that I am not called to understand why You lead me as You do. However, I am called to obey Your direction.

Lord, You chose to make me a special needs' mother. If I had been given a choice, I probably would have declined. It makes me sad to admit that fact because being a mother to these two boys has been such a blessing to me. It hurts my heart to know the things I would have missed out on without them in my life.

God, Your plans for my life and my sons' lives are perfect. You alone know the plan, the reason, and the outcome. Please help me to accept the fact that Your plan is known to You and You will reveal it to me in due time.

Now we see things imperfectly, like puzzling reflections in a mirror, but them we will see everything with perfect clarity. All that I know now is partial and incomplete, but then I will know everything completely, just as God now knows me completely. 1 Corinthians 13:12 NLT

O God,

I am thankful that I do not need to fear the obstacles that get in the way of Your plan for my life. I am trading the old fear that I have carried with me for trust in You. Your perfect love casts out all fear. Please don't allow my fear to stop Your plan for me. Lord, teach me that nothing that happens on this Earth can change or alter Your plan that You have already put in place for me. I understand now that Your plan for me includes being the mother of autistic children.

God, I thank You for everything You do for me. Every bit of progress that my sons make in school is a huge deal to me. I know the good things that happen might seem small to other parents, but I am learning to find joy in small victories. They are triumphs and moments to relish. I no longer aim for perfection. I'm content to just have a day when neither of my children has to be picked up from school for misbehavior. I have learned to praise my children and to celebrate each victory, each step in the right direction, no matter how small.

Thank You for casting out my fear with Your perfect love. Please continue to implement Your plan for my life, God. I am anxious to see what You have in store for me.

There is no fear in love; but perfect love casts out fear. 1 John 4:18a NKJV

O God,

Thank You for being my refuge. Thank You for overlooking my stumbles and instead concentrating on my pursuit of You. Please transform my messy life into a blessed life, something only You can do. I am human, Lord, and I fail You in the way that humans do. Every day, I recognize that I am undeserving of Your grace. I am humbled that You love, guide, comfort, and protect me. Your love is too awesome for words. I cannot express the thankfulness that is in my heart because You pursue me. I know that I am not worthy of Your love, mercy, and grace. However, I am so awed that You bestow them on me nonetheless. Thank You, God, for loving me, a sinner.

Lord, thank You for pursuing my children, too. We take them to church so they can learn about You. I know the depth of Your love for them is great. Lord, I am thankful that You want children to come to You, especially my children. Lord, I feel better about their future knowing that You will always be a place of refuge for them. Please help me to equip them so that as they grow, they will want to know You more and rely upon You.

God is our refuge and strength, always ready to help in times of trouble. So we will not fear when earthquakes come and the mountains crumble into the sea. Psalm 46:1-2 NLT

The Lord is good, a strong refuge when trouble comes. He is close to those who trust in him. Nahum 1:7 NLT

Taste and see that the Lord is good. Oh, the joys of those who take refuge in him! Psalm 34:8 NLT

O my people, trust in him at all times. Pour out your heart to him, for God is our refuge. Psalm 62:8 NLT

O Lord,

I am so thankful that prayer works and that You value my prayers. Some people do not believe prayer works, but I do. I have faith and trust that You will make a difference for me. I know You are not indifferent to my prayers, but that You listen to and answer each one. I am humbled to know that I mean so much to You, that You care enough about me to listen to and answer each of my prayers. Thank you, God, for caring about the details of my life. You are a wonderful God and You direct my steps. I may stumble, but Father, You never let me fall. You are always by me, holding my hand. Thank you, Lord, for Your goodness and love.

God, one of the biggest problems I've had with my son is his inability to swallow the medications that he needs to take to stabilize his behavior. Today, I was blessed by a dear friend who told me that she had not been able to swallow pills even when she was 30 years old! First, that set me off worrying about the future even more. However, she told me that someone had suggested that she use a straw to take a drink after she put the pill in her mouth. She said the pill went right down.

Lord, I immediately went to the store and bought every kind and color of straw available. This evening, I asked my son to try to take his medication using the straw. He was very skeptical, but he agreed to try the straw. Amazingly, the first time he used the straw, he swallowed his medication. I was astonished! I shouldn't have been because, as always, You answered my prayer. You put my friend in my life to tell me her story at exactly the right time. Thank You for caring enough about me to solve this problem and make life better for my family.

The Lord directs the steps of the godly. He delights in every detail of their lives. Though they stumble, they will never fall, for the Lord holds them by the hand. Psalm 37:23-24 NLT

O, Lord, you have examined my heart and know everything about me. You know when I sit down or stand up. You know my thoughts even when I'm far away. You see me when I travel and when I rest at home. You know everything I do. You know what I am going to say even before I say it, Lord. You go before me and follow me. You place your hand of blessing on my head. Such knowledge is too wonderful for me, too great for me to understand. Psalm 139:1-6 NLT

O God,

Help me to trust in You alone and not just in what I hope You will do for me. I choose to trust in You regardless of my circumstances. You have proven You have unlimited resources. Our family had such a great day together at the beach. The boys had fun playing in the water. It was so much like what I think a "normal" family experiences every day. It was especially meaningful to me because our family doesn't have blissful and carefree days like today very often. It makes me appreciate each day that is trouble free.

Teach me to rely on Your understanding and not my own. Help me to acknowledge You in every situation. I invite You to take part in my messy life and to direct my steps. I know that too often I rely on myself and it is so unnecessary for me to do so. You want me to just trust You and to know that You have everything under control. God, I know that You are not going to let me fall, but it doesn't stop me from trying to keep myself upright. Please take that human weakness from me and help me to learn to just put my trust in You.

Trust in the Lord with all your heart and lean not on your own understanding; in all your ways submit to him, and he will make your paths straight. Proverbs 3:5-6 NIV

Dear Jesus,

Help me, please, to stand faithful in all situations, even in the most difficult of times. I know that You will defend and deliver me if I am faithful and place my trust in You. I am learning how to be an advocate for my children by Your example of being an advocate for me. There is so much that You are trying to teach me and sometimes I am slow to learn. I am anxious to get answers to my problems quickly. You want me to be faithful and wait for You to work.

Lord, I have seen You work in my children's lives. It's the simple, little things You have done that show me Your love for them and for me. You have answered my prayers that they would be able to get a haircut without having a full-scale meltdown. Yes, I had to wait for that answer, but You provided. You have answered my prayers that we could clip their nails without them acting like victims of child abuse. You provided an answer to that prayer, also. It wasn't immediately, but the answer came. These are things parents of "normal" children take for granted, but they are answers to prayer for me and I am so thankful for them.

Please search my heart and help me to maintain a pure and contrite heart toward You, regardless of the circumstances of my life. Please give me the patience to learn to wait on You. Thank You for always being my Defender and Deliverer.

Search me, O God, and know my heart; test me and know my anxious thoughts. Psalm 139:23 NLT

Dear God,

Help me to trust in You and not to try to fight my own battles. It only produces fear in me when I try to battle by myself because I know that I am not equipped to win on my own. With Your help, I have won many things for my children. You provided a new doctor that was able to properly diagnose my oldest son and change his medication. His previous medication made him dull and sluggish. He drooled all the time and hardly ever smiled. He seemed practically comatose, with no emotion and no energy. He was just a vacant shell of the child I knew. Now that his medication has changed, he is starting to laugh again and he has a twinkle in his eye. His little personality is shining through and I am so thankful for this victory!

God, I am thankful that I am not alone and that You have promised to always be with me. Thank You for Your promises that are always true. Help me to stand firm upon those promises. Thank You for being a promise-keeping God. Forgive me, Lord, when I have doubted You and not believed in You. Please continue to lead me into the plans and purposes that You have for me as I stand in confident assurance upon Your promises.

But the Lord's plans stand firm forever; his intentions can never be shaken. Psalm 33:11 NLT

You will not have to fight this battle. Take up your positions; stand firm and see the deliverance the Lord will give you, Judah and Jerusalem. Do not be afraid; do not be discouraged. Go out and face them tomorrow, and the Lord will be with you. 2 Chronicles 20:17 NIV

Now it is God who makes both us and you stand firm in Christ. He anointed us, set his seal of ownership on us, and put his spirit in our hearts as a deposit, guaranteeing what is to come. 2 Corinthians 1:21-22 NIV

O God,

I know that I must be patient while waiting on You. Patience is not coming easily to me today. I am so anxious for something positive to happen with my sons. It has been several days in a row of chaos and trouble. It hurts me to see the boys so out of control and angry. They do not even understand why they act the way that they do. They cannot even explain why they are angry. It just hurts on the inside, so it manifests on the outside. They are kicking holes in the wall and ripping up every piece of paper in the house. Their anger makes me fearful and full of hurt at the same time.

Help me to know the work You want me to do while I am waiting for Your answer. Strengthen me in waiting. Lord, I know You have good things in store for me at the right time. Help me to patiently wait for that right time and not to try to make something happen on my own. Thank You for filling my heart and making me aware of Your presence every day.

Wait on the Lord; be of good courage, and He shall strengthen your heart. Wait, I say, on the Lord! Psalm 27:14 NKJV

Be still before the Lord and wait patiently for him. Psalm 37:7a NIV

Dear God,

Today I have felt hopeless, overwhelmed, and full of despair. The children across the street were bullying my son. To make matters worse, their father was standing out there with them and made no effort to make them stop. I don't understand this kind of behavior. Please be my refuge and hiding place. I know that I am weak, but You are strong. I feel awash on the sands of life. Please be my firm foundation.

Lord, when my children are bullied and misunderstood, I do not handle the situation well. People don't understand how difficult life can be for them. A lot of people look at them and see that they look "normal," and they tell me that I need to discipline my kids. It makes me want to lash out at people and tell them that they have no idea what my children need.

God, I know that You are beside me and that You don't want me to condemn the people who are criticizing my children and me. Help me to remember to be the mother You want me to be and to place my cares in Your capable hands because You are my hiding place.

For you are my hiding place; you protect me from trouble. You surround me with songs of victory. Psalm 32:7 NLT

Dear God,

Where are You? I've asked that question many times in the last few weeks. Have You have left me? Can you even hear me when I pray because there seems to be no answer. My despair has become overwhelming. I am at my breaking point. I can't take another uncaring teacher or neighbor or one more night of watching my children have meltdowns. It is crushing my spirit to have so much chaos happening.

God, are You near? I need You to come to my rescue. There is no one else that will provide the lifeline that You extend to me. I was prepared for a short time of struggle, but I didn't know that I would endure a long season of struggle instead. There seems to be no end to this trial. Please rescue me and remind me that You are with me to finish this battle and that You won't leave me until it's resolved.

Please come near to me in these hard times and let me feel Your Spirit. Please console me and strengthen me so that I can endure and overcome these situations. I don't have the strength in myself, but You do and I know You are willing and able to give it to me. Please don't let my faith in You be shaken. I know that when the rain subsides, I will be able to see that You were there with me throughout the storm, holding my hand, and keeping me safe.

The righteous cry out, and the Lord hears them; he delivers them from all their troubles. The Lord is close to the broken-hearted and saves those who are crushed in spirit. The righteous person may have many troubles, but the Lord delivers him from all of them. Psalm 34:17-19 NIV

God is our refuge and our strength, an ever-present help in trouble. Therefore we will not fear, though the earth give away and the mountains fall into the heart of the sea, though its water foam and the mountains quake with their surging. Psalm 46:1 NIV

Let all that I am wait quietly before God, for my hope is in him. He alone is my rock and my salvation, my fortress where I will not be shaken. My victory and honor come from God alone. He is my refuge, a rock where no enemy can reach me. O my people, trust in him at all times. Pour out your heart to him, for God is our refuge. Psalm 62:5-8 NLT

Dear God,

I pray for a friend to come along beside me and to walk with me through this difficult time. I have some really good friends, but they don't live here. I need someone who I can talk to, who will give me hugs, and pray with me. Please send me someone who will pray for my family and who will form a team with me and help me up when I fall from the weight of my burden.

Lord, I know that Satan wants me to feel isolated and all alone on my journey. This is not Your will. I tend to isolate myself because there are so many places I cannot take my children due to their behavior and the reaction of other parents. Even when I am isolated, I know You are my constant companion. Please send me a friend who will walk close beside me and not leave me alone. I know that You have the perfect person in mind who will lift me up in prayer, encourage me, and love my children. I thank You, Lord, for the person You are going to place in my life. You know just who I need.

Two people are better off than one, for they can help each other succeed. If one person falls, the other can reach out and help. But someone who falls alone is in real trouble. A person standing alone can be attacked and defeated but two can stand back-to-back and conquer. Three are even better, for a triple-braided cord is not easily broken. Ecclesiastes 4:10, 12 NLT

Dear God,

I know I have been guilty of asking or expecting You to show me a sign about something in my life. I realize that when I do that, I am challenging You by saying, "If You're really God, then do something." Please do not allow my faith to be based on what I see or feel. I don't want to pursue signs, I want to pursue You.

God, You have picked me up when I've been very down. Just last week, I had a meeting at school with my son's special education committee. At his last school, these meetings were generally unpleasant. It almost seemed like a competition for who could say the worst things about my son and how bad and unruly he was.

However, at this new school, when I walked into the meeting, one of the committee members looked up at me and smiled. She asked, "Do you go to Fellowship Bible Church? I recognize you." A few of the other committee members said they recognized me from church, too. Lord, this meeting had not even started and it was already better than any I had ever attended!

As the meeting progressed and each team member gave her report, I could sense that they were becoming very fond of my son. The speech therapist said when she got his file from the previous school, she was very concerned about working with him because his behavior had been so bad. However, when she met him, she found him to be a sweet child. The entire meeting went well and every person had something positive to say. God, I needed that experience and I thank You and praise You for it.

Lord, teach me patience to wait on Your timing because Your timing is always right. Don't let me get in a hurry. Help me to understand that You may not be answering my prayer right now because You want me to seek You more intensely.

When the Pharisees heard that Jesus had arrived, they came and started to argue with him. Testing him, they demanded that he show them a miraculous sign from heaven to prove his authority. When he heard this, he sighed deeply in his spirit and said, "Why do these people keep demanding a miraculous sign? I tell you the truth, I will not give this generation any such sign. Mark 8:11-12 NLT

O Lord,

I am struggling. There are days when I don't believe I can keep going. I am exhausted and overwhelmed by the problems with my sons. There are constant battles with the school and the boys are becoming almost impossible to control at home. In these times, I know it is most important for me to seek refuge in You. I am so thankful that you are sending your angels to keep watch over me and to hold me up, so that I won't get hurt by life's problems.

I take refuge in Your arms. Please shelter and protect me. Keep me safe. Lord, no matter how tough things get, I know that I can always rely on You for protection and safety. You will give me rest and quiet my soul. You hold out Your strong arms to embrace me. I long to be enveloped in Your strong and secure arms, for that is where I find peace and rest for my soul.

Lord, I pray for protection and safety for my children, too. They can't explain why they feel so angry. They don't know why they feel the urge to destroy things. It breaks my heart to see them so full of pain and to be unable to comfort them. But, Lord, You alone can comfort, protect, and keep them safe.

For He shall give His angels charge over you, to keep you in all your ways. In their hands they shall bear you up, lest you dash your foot against a stone. Psalm 91:11-12 NKJV

Lord, my God, I take refuge in you; save and deliver me from all who pursue me. Psalm 7:1 NIV

Draw near to God and He will draw near to you. James 4:8a NKJV

For in the day of trouble he will keep me safe in his dwelling; he will hide me in the shelter of his sacred tent and set me high upon a rock. Psalm 27:5 NIV

Dear God,

I know that the best way to overcome my troubles and sorrows is to enter Your courts with thanksgiving and praise. I have so much to be thankful for, yet I am too often preoccupied with only the negative things that happen.

Lord, I want to thank You for the kind heart that You have given my son. Most children with autism do not experience empathy and in many ways, this is true of him. However, on many occasions, I have seen him give freely from his heart and it is a beautiful thing. I am in awe of the kindness he showed to a classmate today, especially since no one prompted his behavior.

It's only a few weeks until Christmas, so we told our boys not to ask us to buy them anything else because they would be getting Christmas gifts. Yesterday afternoon, he came home from school and immediately started asking me to buy something. I cut him off in mid-sentence. He said, "it's not for me." He told me a girl in his class lost her backpack and she has to bring her things to school in a Wal Mart bag because her mother only has money for bills. He asked me to buy her a pink backpack that he could take to school and give to her the next day. My husband took him shopping and then he went through my bows and put a big purple bow on the backpack. He could barely sleep last night because he was so excited about giving the gift to his classmate.

God, it was such a blessing to me to see how much my son enjoyed giving to someone else. He has performed many random acts of kindness in his short life, but none that touched me as much as the sweetness of the gift of the pink backpack.

I know that You have been faithful to me and that You have blessed me beyond measure. I want to praise You, not be stuck in my problems. When I try to drag You into the midst of my troubles, I am doubting Your goodness and majesty. I tend to be downhearted when what I should be doing is praising You.

Enter his gates with thanksgiving and his courts with praise: give thanks to him and praise his name. For the Lord is good and his love endures forever; his faithfulness continues through all generations. Psalm 100:4-5 NIV

O God,

I am so thankful for Your faithfulness. I prayed recently for a godly woman to become my friend and walk on this journey with me. Not only did you send me a friend, You sent me two wonderful friends to walk along side of me! They both love my children and have learned all they can about autism so they can help me. These are good friends who sincerely pray for my children and for me. I don't feel all alone anymore because I have friends I can trust to talk to about my children and their problems. They are not judgmental. They wisely counsel me.

You never fail me, Lord. You are constant, steadfast, unwavering, and true. You keep me secure. Satan tempts me to believe that You are inconsistent and that You won't love me if I make mistakes. However, I am so thankful, Father, that You are steadfast and faithful to me always.

For great is your love, higher than the heavens; your faithfulness reaches to the skies. Psalm 108:4 NIV

Two people are better off than one, for they can help each other succeed. If one person falls, the other can reach out and help. But someone who falls alone is in real trouble. A person standing alone can be attacked and defeated but two can stand back-to-back and conquer. Three are even better, for a triple-braided cord is not easily broken. Ecclesiastes 4:10, 12 NLT

Dear God,

You know what I am going through. Days have turned into months full of trouble, discouragement, and fear. There are days when I don't think I can go on. The hurt is too much. I can't handle things on my own. I need You, God. Please, don't let me give up too soon. Lord, You persevered on the cross. You had a commitment to finish to the end. Please give me that kind of strength so that I can finish strong.

Lord, sometimes I feel as though autism is a huge weight on my chest and I cannot move it. It keeps me weighed down and often I can't even breathe because the weight is so strong. God, I am limited, but You are limitless. I need to remember this fact always. I cannot lift the weight myself, but it is nothing for You because You are powerful and You yearn to help me, if only I would ask and stop trying to do everything myself.

Don't be afraid, for I am with you. Don't be discouraged, for I am your God. I will strengthen you and help you. I will hold you up with my victorious right hand. Isaiah 41:10 NLT

Why am I discouraged? Why is my heart so sad? I will put my hope in God! I will praise him again—my Savior and my God! Psalm 42:11 NLT

For our present troubles are small and won't last very long. Yet they produce for us a glory that vastly outweighs them and will last forever. 2 Corinthians 4:14 NLT

Father,

Please teach me to wait for Your promises to be fulfilled in my life. In the world today, we want everything we want and we want it right away. This instantaneous culture is not how You work. Lord, give me the patience to wait. I know from past experience that if I think You are taking too long to answer a prayer, it's only because You are making the answer even better before it arrives.

Lord, I remember when my oldest son started second grade. His teacher was very timid and afraid of him. I prayed for a different teacher and you provided one for him. God, the new teacher was perfect for him. She understood him and worked hard to help him make progress. Even more amazing was that the following year, she moved up to teach third grade and she asked to have my son in her classroom! Lord, I have never had a teacher request to teach my son. What joy that brought to my heart and it made third grade so much easier for him to handle. Thank You for the blessing of this special teacher and for Your goodness in providing exactly who my son needed right when he needed her.

Listen to my voice in the morning, Lord. Each morning, I bring my requests to you and wait expectantly. Psalm 5:3 NLT

God,

Please help me to overcome adversity. I feel that I have so much trouble in my life. Hardly a day goes by that there is not a problem with at least one of my sons. To overcome adversity, I know I need to focus on Your greatness and Your endless love for me. I must turn my negative attitude into one of thankfulness and joy. Teach me to shift the attitude of my heart to hopefulness. Too often, I have allowed myself to wallow in hopelessness and self-pity. It must break Your heart to see me engage in this behavior.

God, I know You have the power to steer me away from bad thoughts and feelings. Lord, too often, I allow Satan to take control of my thoughts and to tell me that You have no plan where my children are concerned. He tries to convince me that You don't care about me and that You don't hear my prayers or care about my children or their pain. God, I know that is not true. Please help me to remain faithful to you.

He said, "The Lord is my rock, my fortress, my deliverer; my God is my rock, in whom I take refuge, my shield, and the horn of my salvation. He is my stronghold, my refuge and my savior—from violent people you save me. 2 Samuel 22:2-3 NIV

Dear God,

Tonight was hard. We are on vacation and everyone's nerves are frayed. The boys are unhappy and out of sorts because they are out of their normal routine. Even though I know that it is hard for them, I am still surprised sometimes at how dysfunctional and uncontrollable they can become.

We finally found a place to eat dinner, but when we sat down, my son started hollering for his chicken tenders "right now" at the top of his lungs. Other customers stared as he continued his tirade and we were powerless to stop him until his food came. Needless to say, we ate as quickly as possible and tried to get out of there before any more harm was done.

I am used to the stares of strangers who think we have bad kids who need discipline and that we are terrible parents. As we made our way through the parking lot to our car, our waitress called out to me. In my rush to leave, I had forgotten my purse. She handed it to me and then surprised me by giving me a hug and asking me if my son had autism. She said she recognized it because she used to work with autistic children. She told me to "hang in" there and it would get better. God, I thank you for sending this woman to identify with what I am going through and to give me words of encouragement.

A word fitly spoken is like apples of gold in settings of silver. Proverbs 25:11 NKJV

Everyone enjoys a fitting reply; it is wonderful to say the right thing at the right time! Proverbs 15:23 NLT

God,

Thank You for my precious gifts—my children. Raising them is unlike any challenge I have ever faced. I know that You will provide me with the tools I need to be a good parent. Thank You for trusting me with these children. Please let me raise them according to Your will and plan. Thank You, Lord, for letting me learn more from them than they will ever learn from me.

Equip me Lord to teach them of Your goodness. Help me to be an example to them. I want them to know You, Lord, and to learn to put their trust in You. Just today, I saw an example of how they trust in You. Both boys keep asking for a baby sister. I've told them repeatedly that having a baby sister is not up to me; it's up to God. I reminded them that they're adopted and God sent both of them to me. I said, "If God wants to send us a baby sister, He will. My oldest son immediately started praying out loud, "God, won't You please send us a baby sister? Thank You. Amen." A few minutes later, he informed me that "God said no, mom."

I want them to have multiple occasions to call upon Your name and to listen for Your answer. Please help them to understand and experience Your love and rely upon You to guide them through the circumstances of life. I want them to understand how important You are in my life. Lord, I know I would not have lasted a single day without Your love and intervention.

Children are a gift from the Lord; they are a reward from him. Psalm 127:3 NLT

O Lord,

I bring to You today my sorrow, sadness, and confusion. I want Your goodness to provide comfort and solace to me. I know that You have been here for me in the past and that You have promised to never leave me or forsake me. God, I know that it is Your desire to comfort me and to keep me through this difficult time. Help me to go boldly before Your throne of grace. Please make sense of my sadness and confusion. Many times, You have brought clarity to me and I pray that You will do so again.

Thank You for the blessings You have given me such as finding the right school for one of my sons and for providing a great friend for my other son. I am most thankful for the special needs' ministry at our church. It gives my husband and me the opportunity to worship each week without being distracted by our children. You have placed wonderful people in this ministry that love all the special needs' children and who really have a heart for this ministry. It has been an enormous blessing to our family. God, You continue to amaze me with the wonderful works You do for my children and I thank You and praise You for it.

May the Lord our God be with us as he was with our ancestors; may he never leave or abandon us. May he give us the desire to do his will in everything and to obey all the commands, decrees, and regulations that he gave our ancestors. 1 Kings 8:57-58 NLT

God,

I am so grateful that You don't give me what I truly deserve. Instead, You freely give me what I don't deserve—Your mercy and grace, and everlasting forgiveness. You are gracious and full of loving kindness. Help me to fear You, Lord. I am in awe of Your mercy, which I know I don't deserve. Teach me to be thankful for the many blessings You place in my life.

You bestowed a blessing on our family just a few nights ago. My husband and I have been so concerned about what will happen to our children as they grow older. Will they be able to get an education? Will they be able to get jobs or live on their own? A few nights ago, a friend of my husband's invited him to dinner. His friend brought along his 18 year-old son who has high-functioning autism like our sons. This friend wanted my husband to have a "glimpse into his future." It was such a blessing to see that this boy had completed high school and was gainfully employed. It gave us so much hope that our sons may similarly have a bright future. Thank You for Your goodness and all that You provide for us.

From the depths of despair, O Lord, I call for your help. Hear my cry, O Lord. Pay attention to my prayer. Lord, if you kept a records of our sins, who, O Lord, could ever survive? But you offer forgiveness that we might learn to fear you. Psalm 130:3-4 NLT

Let all that I am praise the Lord; with my whole heart, I will praise his holy name. Let all that I am praise the Lord; may I never forget the good things he does for me. Psalm 103:1-2 NLT

I will praise you, Lord, with all my heart; I will tell of the marvelous things you have done. I will be filled with joy because of you. I will sing praises to your name, O Most High. Psalm 9:1-2 NLT

Lord,

Please help me with my tendency to be negative. Please give me a joyful mindset, regardless of my circumstances. Help me to be like Peter who could walk on water when he kept his eyes fixed on You. He began to sink when he took his eyes off You. I want to keep my eyes fixed on You and let go of the daily problems and stress. Let me look at my life through Your eyes, by keeping my eyes fixed on You. I know that I sink when I take my eyes off you.

Lord, I don't want to sink. I want to be positive. I want to have joy. Too often, I allow myself to be dragged down by the circumstances surrounding my children. I don't allow myself the luxury of just enjoying the good things that happen with my sons because I'm always fearful that something bad is lurking just around the corner.

Lord, please help me to keep my eyes focused on You and to walk courageously with my gaze fixed on You. I don't want to take my eyes off You and find myself under water. Please teach me to wait patiently for Your answers and for Your plans to be fulfilled in my life.

But Jesus spoke to them at once. "Don't be afraid," he said. "Take courage. I am here!" Then Peter called to him, "Lord, if it's really you, tell me to come to you, walking on the water." "Yes, come," Jesus said. So Peter went over the side of the boat and walked on water toward Jesus. But when he saw the strong wind and the waves, he was terrified and began to sink. "Save me, Lord!" he shouted. Jesus immediately reached out and grabbed him. "You have so little faith," Jesus said. "Why did you doubt me?" Matthew 14:27-31 NLT

Dear God,

My life seems to be falling apart again. There is never any continuity of the good times. One day my children will have a good day and the very next day, everything will go wrong. My sons have been suspended from school again for bad behavior. Their medications don't seem to be keeping them stable. My afterschool caregiver has become unreliable and is probably going to quit. It is so hard to find someone to trust with my children. Everything seems to go wrong at once. I feel helpless, but You know that. You designed me to live my life dependent upon You.

God, I am thankful that You give me challenging times because they are an opportunity to center my faith. I know that You are near me in the midst of my problems, giving comfort to my soul. Thank You for loving me, for listening to my problems, and most of all, for being near to me. I feel Your love all around me in kind words spoken by friends and hugs from other moms. Thank You for always being near when I call upon You and for never leaving me.

The Lord is close to all who call on him, yes, to all who call on him in truth. He grants the desires of those who fear him; he hears their cries for help and rescues them. Psalm 145:18-19 NLT

How long must I wrestle with my thoughts and day after day have sorrow in my heart? How long will my enemy triumph over me? But I trust in your unfailing love; my heart rejoices in your salvation. I will sing the Lord's praise, for he has been good to me. Psalm 1:2, 5-6 NIV

No one will be able to stand against you all the days of your life. As I was with Moses, so I will be with you; I will never leave you nor forsake you. Joshua 1:5 NIV

Dear Lord,

I want my life to count for something for You. I want it to represent great faith in You. I don't want to live a life of fear, missing opportunities You have provided for me. Make me strong, Lord, so that my life means something for eternity. Lord, I am not asking for fame and fortune, just for my faith in You to shine forth. Lord, if I make Your name great, I will have made much of my life.

Lord, please use me for something great for Your kingdom and glory. Please use the gifts You have blessed me with to make a difference in this world so that You will be glorified. Please use my circumstances of raising autistic children to help other special needs' parents and to give them hope and encouragement. I want to be able to convey to other families the wonderful blessings You have bestowed upon my family. Although we go through trying circumstances, You are always there to love and comfort us.

So, my dear brothers and sisters, be strong and immovable. Always work enthusiastically for the Lord, for you know that nothing you do for the Lord is ever useless. 1 Corinthians 15:58 NLT

O God,

Thank You for encouraging me. You are so good to me. This morning on the radio, I heard a beautiful song called "Even If." I felt that You sent the song right to my heart just when I needed it. The words of the song said that even if the healing doesn't come, life falls apart, and dreams are left undone, You are God, You are good, ever faithful One. Those words spoke truth to me. Many times I have prayed for You to heal my sons and make them "normal." Through the words of this song, You encouraged me that You are faithful and still a great and mighty God even if my prayers are not answered in the way I would like them to be.

Many times I have prayed for You to remove the circumstances that complicate and disorder my life. Instead, You encourage me. Your grace is sufficient for me and Your power is made perfect in my weakness. Lord, thank You for encouraging me to grow in character, instead of making my life problem-free. Lord, my most difficult moments have forged my spirit to become stronger and more reliant on You. Thank You, Lord, for hearing my cries and being attentive to me when I am in need.

You, Lord, hear the desire of the afflicted; you encourage them, and you listen to their cry. Psalm 10:17 NIV

But he said to me, "My grace is sufficient for you, for my power is made perfect in weakness." Therefore, I will boast all the more gladly about my weaknesses, so that Christ's power may rest on me. 2 Corinthians 12:9 NIV

Dear God,

I am thankful that I know You and that You know me. Lord, You know my name! I am important to You! That is such a wonderful truth. God, I would rather be known by You than by anyone on earth. Lord, I am thankful to know You and not just know about You. Lord, with You on my side, no situation, no problem, and no circumstance can defeat me. When life makes me feel down-hearted and hope seems to be slipping away, I know that perception is only in my eyes. You are in control and I will let my faith guide me so that You can make the impossible, possible.

Lord, I have seen first-hand Your ability to make the impossible become possible. There is no denying the joy and fulfillment my sons have brought into my life. I have seen them do things that I never thought would be possible. I remember the first time my oldest son decided to ride his bicycle without training wheels. I saw pure joy on his face when he rode down the street for the first time on two wheels! Another time, he was able to learn a few lines for a play and participate along with the other children in his class. Your goodness is overwhelming. Thank You for knowing me and caring about me and my family.

"Be strong and courageous! Don't be afraid or discouraged because of the king of Assyria or his mighty army, for there is a power far greater on our

side! He may have a great army, but they are merely men. We have the Lord our God to help us and to fight battles for us!" 2 Chronicles 32:7-8a NLT

Be on your guard; stand firm in the faith; be courageous; be strong. 1 Corinthians 16: 13 NIV

Dear God,

Sometimes when I pray for something, I expect a specific result and I question You when things don't turn out the way I had hoped. I know this is wrong, Lord. I must submit to Your plans and let You direct the way that I should proceed. I am thankful that You always have a plan and that You have guided me in ways that have helped my children.

You have opened doors for them that I never could have done on my own. You provided an overnight camp for them to attend with other children with special needs. This experience was so good for them because they got to enjoy going to camp just like "normal" kids. It also provided a needed respite for my husband and me. Another time, You provided a summer day camp for them to enjoy with other special needs' children. God, You are so good.

You know everything about the future and how all the events of my life are orchestrated to produce just the right result at just the right time. God, help me to remain unshakable in the midst of life's problems and to allow Your Holy Spirit to guide me to the victory that You intend for me.

But the Lord's plans stand firm forever: his intentions can never be shaken.
Psalm 33:11 NLT

Dear God,

I feel sad and discouraged today, Lord. Just when I think things are improving, something unexpected happens with one of the boys. At school yesterday, one of my sons ran out of the building when a parent came in to teach the children how to send a message in a balloon. He is so terrified of the sound that a popping balloon makes. His sensory issues make the sound of a popping balloon sound like a shotgun is going off in his ear. I had trouble getting the teacher to understand this. She could only see that he ran out of the class and out of the building without permission.

The constant turmoil threatens my peace of mind. I find my patience fleeing. Stop me from trying to be self-sufficient. I need Your help. At these times, encourage me to recall Your promises and Your faithfulness. Allow Your Holy Spirit to speak to my soul and to drown out all the noise of the world around me. Then I will be able to praise You.

Why, my soul, are you downcast? Why so disturbed within me? Put your hope in God, for I will yet praise him, my Savior and my God. Psalm 43:5 NIV

Lord,

I am so thankful that I can *always* call upon You for help. You are constant, always available, and reliable—all of the time. You never tell me "later," or "not now." You are my ever-present help in times of trouble. There is no situation or struggle that is too great for You to overcome.

God, tonight I took my oldest son to the try-outs for Upward Basketball. Every child gets to play, so the try-outs are more to assess skill level so that the teams are fairly balanced in terms of ability. He didn't know this fact, though. He was excited to try-out, but worried that he would not make the team.

He was put in a group of five boys and the first drill required the boys to dribble around some cones that were set up on the gym floor. I watched as my son began the drill. He tried so hard, but it was painful to watch. He couldn't weave in and out of the cones while dribbling. His motor skill development just didn't allow it. More than once, his ball rolled away, but he didn't quit. He kept retrieving his ball and starting over.

All the drills went about the same. He just couldn't do what most of the other kids could do due to his lack of coordination. I was so proud of him, though, because he didn't get angry and he didn't quit. Part of me wanted to rush over and tell the "coach," to give my son a break because he had autism. The other part of me just wanted to cry. In fact, my eyes filled with tears a few times when he was struggling with the drills. Most of the other parents weren't even paying attention because they knew their children could perform the drills.

After the drills were done, my son found the man who had been testing him and tapped him on the shoulder. He asked, "Coach, did I make it? Did I make the team?" This man turned and looked at my son's big, wondering eyes, patted him on the back, and said very kindly, "You sure did, buddy. You sure did make the team!" My son began jumping and dancing and making his happy noises. God, I was so thankful that this man took that extra little bit of time to make my son feel special. God, please teach me to give every situation to You and to trust in Your steadfast love.

Rise up and help us; rescue us because of your unfailing love. Psalm 44:26 NIV

Dear Lord,

I feel so sad when I see my son longing for a friend. He can relate to adults or to very young children, but he has no idea how to relate to a child his own age. I have seen other children take advantage of him by promising to be his friend if he gives them one of his toys or some money. He thinks "buying" a friend is normal. My heart aches so much, Lord, when I learn that he has given away his new toy or part of his allowance so that another child will be his "friend."

Lord, last night, he prayed again for *just one friend*. I am so thankful it was dark in his room so that he couldn't see the tears that glistened in my eyes when he said that. Lord, I know that You can answer prayers and so I prayed then that You would send him that friend.

Tonight, we were eating dinner when the doorbell rang. I answered the door and a boy who lives down the street was standing there with a basketball and asked if my son could come out to play. Lord, I thanked You silently in my heart for this child and what this small gesture would mean to my son. I called my son and told him that a boy down the street was asking for him to play. Lord, his smile brought tears to my eyes. As he went out the door, he said, "God sent me a friend!" Thank You, Lord Jesus for sending friends to us when we are in need.

I took my troubles to the Lord; I cried out to him, and he answered my prayer. Psalm 17:6 NLT

Be still in the presence of the Lord, and wait patiently for him to act. Psalm 37:7 NLT

Dear God,

My heart is broken today. God, the pastor said that we are never closer to Your heart than when we are broken-hearted. I pray that he is right. We had to send our son to a special program to get help for his problems. The house is so empty without him. I feel guilty that he is not at home, yet his problems were tearing our family apart. I want him to get help and we are not equipped to help him the way that trained professionals can.

Lord, I pray that You would keep him safe; that You would heal his hurts. I pray for peace about this difficult decision. I know that some people judge me for not being able to keep my son at home, but God, I love him so much that I want him to get help so that his life can be better in the future.

God, I know that I will not always be here for him as he grows older, so I want him to gain the skills that he will need to have when I am no longer on this earth. I know that You will always be there beside him, Lord, and that gives me comfort. Lord, I pray that he will know You and put his trust in You. Lord, please wrap Your arms securely around him and keep him safe in Your love.

He heals the brokenhearted and bandages their wounds. Psalm 147:3 NLT

The Lord is close to the brokenhearted and saves those who are crushed in spirit. Psalm 34:18 NLT

Dear God,

I know that there are times when I say that I trust in You, yet I still search for what man can do for me. I still have stress and anxiety which should not be present if I really trusted in You. Lord, I want to live a life of confidence in You. I don't want my struggles and trials to leave me weak in faith and lacking in confidence. Regardless of what is happening in my life, I want to be like a tree with deep roots. I want to have the confidence that the world cannot affect Your purpose for my life. I want to face my future with boldness and not with fear. I place my life in Your hands. My confidence in You cannot be shaken. It cannot be taken away from me.

Help me to understand that I have troubles in my life so that I will remember to rely on You and not on my own strength. Lord, I recognize my battles and my struggles and doing so encourages me to have even more faith in You. God, I am not equipped to fight my own battles, even though sometimes I think I know better than You or feel that You are not working fast enough for me. I am so thankful that You are always there for me, even when I make mistakes, or when I have doubts.

Lord, I struggled with doubt today when my son was sent to alternative school. It's not an appropriate place for children with disabilities. It's a school for children with behavioral problems. I know my son has behavioral problems, but they result from his disabilities. The school does not see it that way and so my son is being shuffled off to another school where he has no chance of success. I know this reassignment will only bring more trouble into my future, but I surrender it to You, Lord. Please help me through my seasons of struggle and moments of pain. I know You are on my side, taking my hand, and guiding me to the joy that comes on the other side of hurt. I am so thankful to not be walking through life alone.

Weeping may last through the night, but joy comes with the morning. Psalm 30:5b NLT

I have told you all this so that you may have peace in me. Here on earth you will have many trials and sorrows. But take heart, because I have overcome the world. John 16:33 NLT

Dear God,

I seem to get discouraged so easily. I try to find activities for my children to participate in, but the result is always the same. They don't sit quietly, they don't follow directions, they don't always listen to the adults. Sometimes, they are mean to the other children. Always when I go to pick them up, I am told that they cannot return to the activity, that it is not appropriate for them, or that other parents have complained about their behavior. God, even at church, I have experienced another mother insisting that my son not be in her son's class.

God, I know You made these children and that You have a plan for them. Please help me, O Lord, to trust You and to make it through these disappointments. Please take away the hurt that I feel at these times when my children are excluded. Please erase their pain also and give us faith to understand that everything that happens is part of Your plan.

God blesses those who patiently endure testing and temptation. Afterwards they will receive the crown of life that God has promised to those who love him. James 1:12 NLT

Dear Lord,

Please give me more patience. Sometimes, it is hard for me to show my children the patience that they deserve. There are days that I go deep into self-pity and feel angry at them for doing things that they can't even help doing. Even then, I know that I'm not really mad at them. I am mad at myself for not being kind and patient, gifts that You willingly bestow on me. Lord, please lift me from the despair that sometimes overcomes me as I deal with the problems my children encounter. Give me the desire and the patience to seek Your help and the patience to wait for it.

Always be humble and gentle. Be patient with each other, making allowance for each other's faults because of your love. Make every effort to make yourselves united in the Spirit, binding yourselves together with peace. Ephesians 4: 2-3 NLT

Rejoice in our confident hope. Be patient in trouble, and keep on praying. Romans 12:12 NLT

Whoever is patient has great understanding, but one who is quick-tempered displays folly. Proverbs 14:29 NIV

Patient endurance is what you need now, so that you will continue to do God's will. Then you will receive all that he has promised. Hebrews 10:36 NLT

Dear God,

I am so amazed about something that happened today because it showed me how much You are working in the life of my children. One of our neighbors, who my sons called Mr. Dale died unexpectedly. He used to drive by our house every morning and honk and wave at my oldest son while he waited for the school bus. We knew it would be hard to explain to him that Mr. Dale had died.

My husband got the task of explaining Mr. Dale's death to our oldest son who is only seven years old. He told our son that Mr. Dale had died and gone to heaven. Our son asked, "Does that mean he gets one of those new bodies in heaven like they talk about in church?" My husband told him that it did, and he said, "That's not fair. I want to get one of those!"

Together they walked down the street to Mr. Dale's house where a large group of family and friends had gathered. Our son gave Mr. Dale's wife a big hug and for a time, he managed to cheer up everyone in the room. As they walked back to our house, my husband wanted to make sure that our son was clear about what had happened to Mr. Dale. He asked our son, "You understand that we won't be seeing Mr. Dale anymore, right?" Our son replied, "No, dad. We'll see him again." My husband started explaining death once again, but our son interrupted him and said, "Dad, won't we see Mr. Dale when *we* go to heaven? So, we will see him again, won't we?" My husband assured him that we would.

Lord, I was delighted and amazed to know that our son had learned so much in church and that he understood about going to heaven when we die. Thank You for opening his heart to hear, understand, and believe Your Word.

The unfolding of your words gives light; it gives understanding to the simple. Psalm 119:130 NIV

But grow in the grace and knowledge of our Lord and Savior Jesus Christ. To him be glory both now and forever! Amen. 2 Peter 3:18 NIV

O God,

Thank You for Your many blessings in my life and for the blessings yet to come. I have felt Your comfort in a mighty way today. I was able to give my son a birthday party and other children came and everyone had a great time. There were no meltdowns or problems with sharing. It was a successful party and we haven't experienced very many parties that went well.

Lord, I want to share Your blessings with others and to be a blessing to them. Just as You give us comfort so that we can comfort others, I know my blessings are given to me so that I can bless others. Lord, I pray that by sharing my story of what You have done in my life, I can encourage others to trust in You when they are in a similar situation.

Give thanks to the Lord and proclaim his greatness. Let the whole world know what he has done. Psalm 105:1 NLT

He comforts us in all our troubles so that we can comfort others. When they are troubled, we will be able to give them the same comfort that God has given us. 1 Corinthians 1:4 NLT

Dear God,

I thank You for the gift of this day because You made it and You gave it to me to live. You want me to rejoice in it. I wonder, Lord, how many of my days could have gone differently if I would have lived like I believed each day was a gift. How many times could I have allowed joy and gladness to overcome doubt, fear, and complaining? God, not only is this day a gift, but my entire life is a gift. Help me to listen to what You are saying to me and to take appropriate actions. I want to listen to and obey Your voice, not shut it out.

I thank You for providing a mentor for my son in his special needs' kindergarten class. A high school student volunteered to work with my son. He showed him how to write down the time, using numerals and a colon. My son didn't get frustrated when he couldn't write everything perfectly. His mentor was so patient and kind with him. My son told everyone about his new friend who was in high school and who is "taller than daddy." These short visits made such a difference in my son's life. They helped him to control his behavior so he could meet with his new friend at the end of each school day. Thank You for sending people into my son's life that pour their lives into him and care about him. You are a marvelous God.

This is the day the Lord has made. We will rejoice and be glad in it. Psalm 118:24 NLT

For you are great and do marvelous deeds; you alone are God. Psalm 86:10 NLT

Father,

Please do not let me forget that I am a child of God. When going through testing and trials, please strengthen my faith. Help me to realize that many of my troubles and sorrows are brought about by my own poor decisions and because I rely on myself too much. Help me to remember that You are my Heavenly Father and that I am a child of the King! God, I am thankful that You are bigger and far stronger than anyone or anything that can come against me.

I can feel Your victory in my life today. Tonight, I watched my son help another child at karate. No one told him to help the child; he just did it out of natural kindness. The other boy has Down Syndrome, but that didn't make any difference to my son. He just saw another child struggling and tried to show him what to do. I was so proud of him and so thrilled that he was showing kindness to another special needs' family. Also, he was so proud of himself for helping someone. Watching that happen made my heart sing.

See what great love the Father has lavished on us, that we should be called children of God! And that is what we are! The reason the world does not know us is that it did not know him. 1 John 3:1 NIV

Dear God,

Tonight was very rough. My son was raging like a wild animal. Lord, I don't know what hurts him so inside. Sadly, I don't think he knows either. Like many other nights, I survey the damage. Holes kicked in walls, papers strewn around the floor, broken dishes, and furniture laying on its side. Lord, this is the ugly part of my life that I don't want anyone to see. It looks picture-perfect on the outside, but inside it's a huge mess. Thankfully, no one was hurt tonight.

Lord, I silently pray to You as these events occur. I don't want them to happen, but they happen nonetheless and I am powerless to stop them. It sometimes feels as though I'm living through a tornado, which has spun into action with no warning. It happens so quickly and then when things get calm, I look around at the damage. I talk to my son who is so sorry, so ashamed, so bewildered about what he has done and why. I cry, Lord, because I am anguished by his torment. I try to comfort him. I pray for You to help him.

God, I am so thankful that You taught me long ago not to consider my earthly possessions to be my treasure. I have been sad when sentimental items have been broken, but I know that my real treasure is in heaven and that it is safe in Your arms.

Don't store up treasures on earth, where moths eat them and rust destroys them, and where thieves break in and steal. Store your treasures in heaven, where moths and rust cannot destroy, and thieves do not break in and steal. Wherever your treasure is, there the desires of your heart will also be. Matthew 6: 19-21 NLT

Dear Lord,

This afternoon the doorbell rang and it was my neighbor from across the street. I wasn't expecting him, but I invited him in anyway. He refused to come in and he said he was just there to tell me that he did not want my children to come to his house or to play with his children again. He said that my sons had problems and he did not want his children exposed to them. Lord, he made it sound as though he thought autism was contagious and his children might catch it if they were around my sons.

God, I know I just stood there for a moment in shock and then I told him, "I guess it is a good thing that God put all of the special children on this side of the street and gave you the perfect children." Then I shut the door in his face because I didn't want him to see me cry. God, I am thankful that You gave me the children with problems because everyone is not willing to become equipped to deal with them.

Lord, I am not proud of myself for being rude to him. I hurt for my children because so many people in this world see them in the same way he did---bad kids that need discipline. They cannot see the goodness in my sons because they are only looking at what they do wrong and not at all the things they do right. Lord, I know my children struggle every day because of their special needs. God, I know that You created them that way, so I ask that You make them strong enough to withstand the hurtful comments of others. God, please give me strength to endure as well.

Work at living in peace with everyone, and work at living a holy life, for those who are not holy will not see the Lord. Hebrews 12: 14 NLT

Give your burdens to the Lord, and he will take care of you. He will not permit the godly to slip and fall. Psalm 55:22 NLT

Never pay back evil with more evil. Do things in such a way that everyone can see you are honorable. Do all that you can to live in peace with everyone. Dear friends, never take revenge. Leave that to the righteous anger of God. For the scriptures say, "I will take revenge; I will pay them back," says the Lord. Romans 12: 17-19 NLT

Dear God,

I confess that for the longest time, I have prayed for You to heal my children, to just make them "normal," so they can fit in, have friends, and enjoy things that other children their ages enjoy. Looking back, I wonder sometimes how much I wanted the "healing" for me instead of them. Was I the one longing for the normalcy instead of the pain and sorrow?

I've come to realize that I am the one lacking faith. How sad it must have made You for me to ask You to change Your creation into something more acceptable. What You create, Father, is perfect. It doesn't need healing or changes or adjustments to make it "normal." You create only the perfect, the beautiful, and the majestic. True, it would have made my life more convenient if You had created my sons differently, but I would have missed out on so much that You intended for me to learn.

Lord, as I see my sons grow up and mature, I am thankful for the young men they are becoming. They have endured a lot of pain and sadness, but they are strong. You gave them supportive parents and godly friends and mentors. You have surrounded and embraced them with Your love everyday of their lives and I know that You constantly watch over them.

Thank you, Lord, for blessing my life with Your two perfect creations. Help me, Lord, to be the best mother to them that I can possibly be. Thank you, Lord, for Your goodness to our family.

The secret things belong to the Lord our God, but the things which are revealed belong to us and to our children, forever, that we may do all the words of this law. Deuteronomy 29:29 NKJV

As you do not know the path of the wind or how the body is formed in the womb, so you cannot understand the work of God, the maker of all things. Ecclesiastes 11:5 NIV

Dear God,

I say I trust in You and yet I find that I tend to rely on myself to get me through situations. What I am really doing is trusting in my own abilities. I get impatient because You are not acting fast enough for me or in the way that I think You should. When my children are hurting, I want the hurt to stop immediately. I don't want them to endure pain. I want to take it all away from them and endure it myself. I want You to make it stop! I want You to take away their pain.

I know that to have the faith and trust in You that I need, I must totally surrender to You. I can't keep my hand on the steering wheel. I can't keep trying to rig the outcome to be what I want it to be. I can't be afraid of losing something or someone. I am vulnerable and afraid because I try to keep too much control over things in my life, especially my children. I want to fully surrender to You so that I have nothing to fear. I know that my fear is the result of not fully surrendering my life and my family to You.

Those who trust in the Lord are as secure as Mount Zion; they will not be defeated but will endure forever. Psalm 125:1 NIV

Dear God,

Please help my children to see themselves through Your eyes. Many days they believe they are less than other people. They see only their faults, their issues, their failures, their problems. They fail to see their successes, the joy they bring to others, their kind acts. Instead, they see themselves in ways You never intended. You view them as the perfect creations You made.

Lord, if only they could see themselves through Your eyes. If they could understand the value You placed on their lives when You breathed them into existence. If they could grasp the purpose You have for their lives, it would open the world to them. Please help them to understand that You created them intentionally—just the way they are—and that You did it for purposes perhaps too great for them to fathom. And, Lord, I pray that you would use their lives for Your glory.

See what great love the Father has lavished on us, that we should be called children of God! And that is what we are. The reason the world does not know us is that it did not know him. Dear friends, now we are children of God, and what we will be has not yet been made known. But we know that when Christ appears, we shall be like him, for we shall see him as he is. 1 John 3:1-2 (NIV)

But you are a chosen people, a royal priesthood, a holy nation, God's special possession, that you may declare the praises of him who called you out of darkness into wonderful light. 1 Peter 2:9 NIV

You didn't choose me. I chose you. I appointed you to go and produce lasting fruit, so that the Father will give you whatever you ask for, using my name. John 15:16 NLT

Dear Lord,

It breaks my heart to hear my children pray for "just one friend." Lord, it brings back memories of me praying for "just one baby" when I couldn't get pregnant. Father, You had a plan then. You sent me the children that You wanted me to have through the miracle of adoption.

I didn't understand Your plan then. I waited for four years and I was not patient. I kept on asking and asking instead of being still and listening to what You were trying to tell me. I was like a child at Christmas, asking You for things, when You already had my gifts purchased and hidden in the top of the closet. You had not, one, but two babies for me—brothers—that You gave to me in Your perfect time. I know that You will provide friends for my children, too.

A man of many companions may come to ruin, but there is a friend who sticks closer than a brother. Proverbs 18:24 ESV

Father,

You are a solid rock rising tall in the depths of the ocean. When the waves of life are blowing me about, You draw me to stand on Your rock and You shelter me. When life is calm, I can swim around Your rock, being content in Your peace. Sometimes the water is so calm and so low that I feel empowered to swim away, certain that I can survive on my own and make decisions without Your help.

However, just as suddenly, storms gather and the water rises to dangerous levels, and I struggle to find my way back to You. Lord, I am so thankful that You are a solid rock that never moves. When I am in need, You are always there, always beckoning me to You. Whether the waters are calm or treacherous, You stand ready to lift me out of the waves and to protect me from harm.

O God, listen to my cry! Hear my prayer! From the ends of the earth, I cry to you for help when my heart is overwhelmed. Lead me to the towering rock of safety. Psalm 61:1-2 NLT

I cried out, "I am slipping!" but your unfailing love, O Lord, supported me. When doubts filled my mind, your comfort gave me renewed hope and cheer. Psalm 94:18-19 NLT

But the Lord is my fortress; my God is the mighty rock where I hide. Psalm 94:22 NLT

Dear God,

Please help me to see my children through Your eyes. Give me the capacity to see their value to You and to know how You intend to use them for Your kingdom. Help me to instill that value in them. Lord, please do not let me be grieved when others see my children as something less than You intended.

Please remind me, God, that my children are like David to You. When others looked at David, they saw only a shepherd boy, but when You looked at David, You saw a king. Thank You, Lord, for not seeing shepherd boys when You look at my children. Thank You for seeing kings in them also.

But the Lord said to Samuel, "Do not look on his appearance or on the height of his stature, because I have rejected him. For the Lord sees not as man sees; man looks on the outward appearance, but the Lord looks at his heart." 1 Samuel 16:7 NKJV

Dear God,

I must confess that I was happy and relieved the morning I went outside and found a "for sale" sign in my neighbor's yard. It has been hard living across the street from people who found my children inferior and who did not want their children to associate with mine. At times, even the father bullied my oldest son or simply stood by in silence as his children did. So, I am thankful that they moved because it made some of the hurt go away from my heart.

But God, I am even more thankful for the new family that moved into their house. It wasn't just any family. It was a special family—the one from our previous neighborhood whose son asked to play with mine when he prayed for "just one friend." God, I can see Your hand so clearly in this situation and I thank You, Lord Jesus, for Your marvelous plan and provision.

Just as you cannot understand the path of the wind or the mystery of a tiny baby growing in its mother's womb, so you cannot understand the activity of God, who does all things. Ecclesiastes 11:5 NLT

How great is our Lord! His power is absolute! His understanding is beyond comprehension. Psalm 147:5 NLT

Father,

Thank You, God for answering a prayer that my son has been praying for weeks. During our summer vacation, there had been a big storm and afterwards, there was an enormous rainbow in the sky. My son loved that rainbow because he knew the story of Noah, but he had never seen such a gorgeous rainbow before. Every night in his prayers, he has asked You for a rainbow. I always remind him that it has to rain first and then we can look for a rainbow.

This evening we had our community group from church over to our house for dinner. All the children were playing outside. My oldest son burst into the house, yelling with excitement that there was a rainbow. He said, "There's a rainbow! There's a rainbow! I knew God would send me a rainbow because I prayed for it!"

Lord, I looked out the window and there was bright sunshine just as there had been all day. I doubted there was a rainbow because there had been no rain. My son insisted that not only was there a rainbow, but it was in our backyard. His excitement was so contagious that all the adults went outside to look. As we stepped outside on the deck, we were stopped in our tracks by the sight of the biggest and most beautiful rainbow we had ever seen—and it did appear to be right in our backyard. There were no adults with dry eyes.

God, I pray to have the faith of my son who could not contain himself from exclaiming over and over again that You had answered his prayer and sent him a rainbow. Lord, I realized something important that day. My son had faith that You would answer his prayer. I don't always have that faith, Lord, but I want to.

"You don't have enough faith," Jesus told them, "I tell you the truth, if you had faith even as small as a mustard seed, you could say to this mountain, 'Move from here to there' and it would move. Nothing would be impossible. Matthew 17:20 NLT

And we are confident that he hears us whenever we ask for anything that pleases him. And since we know he hears us when we make our requests, we also know that he will give us what we ask for. 1 John 5:14-15 NLT

And Jesus answered them, "Truly, I say to you, if you have faith and do not doubt, you will not only do what has been done to the fig tree, but even if you say to this mountain, 'Be taken up and thrown into the sea,' it will happen. And whatever you ask in prayers, you will receive, if you have faith. Matthew 21: 21-22 ESV

Dear God,

As a mother, I have tried to teach my children to pray at night before they go to bed. My oldest son loves to pray. I confess to being somewhat envious of his relationship with You. Lord, I love how he prays straight from his heart. No matter what is on his mind—happy or sad, serious or humorous, he talks to You about it as though the two of you are the best of friends. Not only that, Lord, he fully believes that You hear and answer his prayers. His faith is astonishing at times.

It amuses me to hear him pray and ask You to keep away the "bad guy that lives under the street." That is his description of Satan. I always picture a red-horned demon peering out through the manhole cover, searching to find my son. I am thankful that he does not want Satan to be near him.

Lord, I love how he always starts off his prayer by saying, "Thank you for me." In my life, it has never once occurred to me to thank You for making me. One night I asked him why he included that line in his prayers. He said, "Since you told me that God made me special, I want to give him thanks for making me that way because it probably took extra work."

God, I am overcome by my son's thankfulness to You and his extraordinary faith in Your ability to answer his prayers. Lord, I need to express that degree of gratitude and faith. Thank You for sending me a child to teach me this important lesson.

Be thankful in all circumstances, for this is God's will for you who belong to Christ Jesus. 1 Thessalonians 5:18 NLT

How precious are your thoughts about me, O God. They cannot be numbered! I can't even count them; they outnumber the grains of sand! And when I wake up, you are still with me. Psalm 139:17-18 NLT

Dear God,

I know that people mean well when they say "God gives special children to special parents." However, I know that is not the case. There is nothing "special" about my husband or me. In us, You chose ordinary people who were willing to be obedient to Your will. We had no "special" qualities when You gave us these children, nor do we possess any now. We are just ordinary people equipped by You.

Lord, I am thankful that You decided to use us to raise these children. I am so grateful that, in Your wisdom, You choose to use ordinary people to do extraordinary things, empowered by You. I pray that I will continue to be obedient to Your will so that I can be the mother that You want me to be. Help me to trust in You completely to do the work that You have called me to do. Please give me the strength and desire to be the best mother I can possibly be.

The Lord is my strength and my shield. My heart trusts in him and I am helped. Therefore, my heart exults, and with my son, I thank him. Psalm 28:7 NAS

But the Lord stood with me and gave me strength. 2 Timothy 4:17a NLT

For God is working in you, giving you the desire and the power to do what pleases him. Philippians 2:13 NLT

Dear God,

I am so thankful for my children and that You picked them just for me. Lord, I've spent countless hours praying for them and I hope that someday they will know and understand that and do the same when they have children of their own. I haven't let a day go by that I don't pray for their safety and well-being, their happiness, and my hopes for their success in life.

It is such a comfort to me to know that no matter how hard the day has been and that no matter what problems my children or I have encountered that day, I can take it all to You in prayer. You give me peace. You tell me that You have it under control. You tell me to lay it at Your feet and not to worry. Thank You, God. I learned a long time ago that I could not handle this situation on my own and I am so thankful that You are here to carry the load, to ease the pain, and to love me.

So do not fear, for I am with you; do not be dismayed, for I am your God. I will strengthen you and help you; I will uphold you with my righteous right hand. Isaiah 41:10 NIV

Dear God,

When storms rage in my life, it doesn't matter how fiercely the winds blow or how high the waves get, it never comes as a surprise to You, God. You are not alarmed or in a panic. Things are going exactly the way You planned. Today was a particularly stormy day. No one could tell me exactly why my son had a major meltdown at school today, but it was huge. First, a teacher saw him throw an opened milk carton across the cafeteria. When she tried to talk to him, he ran from her, but she caught him, and he started hitting her with his lunchbox.

Next, he went back into the cafeteria and with his hands "swept" several filled lunch trays off the cafeteria tables and onto the floor. The teacher caught him again and took him to her classroom where he began kicking her and throwing magnets she had in her room. He ran out of the room again and hid in the bathroom. Two teachers found him and he hit one of them. The other teacher managed to get him to the principal's office and left him there while she went to find the principal. While in there alone, he locked both office doors from the inside and knocked every item and paper he could find to the floor. A teacher finally got the door unlocked, but he ran out and started to hit and kick the teacher who grabbed him. His teacher and aide were finally able to calm him down.

I know storms like this will continue to come into my life, so teach me to rely on Your strength to face these storms. Help me not to wonder where You are when trouble and chaos abound. I am tired of trying to weather the storms of life on my own. I want and need Your power and strength to face each storm. Teach me to turn to You first and to patiently endure the hard times. Help me to praise You in the midst of the storms and to hold firmly to You.

Lord, you are my strength and my fortress, my refuge in the day of trouble!
Jeremiah 16:19 NLT

Call upon Me in the day of trouble; I will deliver you, and you shall glorify
Me. Psalm 50:15 NKJV

Dear God,

When my children were little, I felt such incredible pain when they hurt. Now that they are teenagers, it is even worse, if that's possible. Now they are old enough to understand when other people are being mean to them or making fun of them. They feel the pain of being excluded from social gatherings or left out of activities. They want to belong, to have friends, and to not be different.

Lord, I worry because sometimes they say that they don't even want to live. I know the pain has to be excruciating for them to even give voice to such thoughts. God, I can't even imagine the heartache I would feel if they ever acted on such feelings. I try to reassure them about all the positive things in their lives. They both have extraordinary things about them. I try to encourage them to see themselves through Your eyes and not through their own lens. Lately, however, it is becoming harder and harder to convince them of their value to You, to our family, and to society.

God, please give me the words to say that will make a difference to them. I know they are frustrated when they compare themselves to other teenagers and find themselves lacking. Lord, I pray that they will rely on You. It is something I have taught them to do all their lives, but as they have grown older, it is harder for them to do, which make me very sad. Their faith is tested as they struggle to understand why You created them as You did.

Lord, I know that You will reveal Your plan to them one day and they will finally understand why You created them as You did. Until that time, I pray that You will hold them safely and securely in Your arms. Speak to them and tell them that they are loved and they are precious in Your sight.

The eyes of the Lord watch over those who do right; his ears are open to their cries for help. The Lord hears his people when they call to him for help. He rescues them from all their troubles. Psalm 34: 15, 17 NLT

How long must I struggle with anguish in my soul, with sorrow in my heart every day? How long will my enemy have the upper hand? Turn and answer me, O Lord, my God! Restore the sparkle to my eyes, or I will die. Don't let my enemies gloat saying, "We have defeated him!" Don't let them rejoice at my downfall. Psalm 13:2-4 NLT

Father,

I've prayed so many times for You to take away the heartache and pain that autism has brought into my life and that of my family. I am finally starting to realize that You haven't taken away the struggles, the pain, or the heartaches of autism because You are using them in ways I could have never imagined.

You have used autism to teach me unconditional love and patience, to help me find joy where I thought there was none. You have shown me how to be content when life is chaotic. But, mostly, Lord, You have used autism to draw me closer to You, to cause me to seek You, to pray to You, and to rely on You. Autism has caused me to take my relationship with You to a much deeper level than ever before. I am so thankful that I can stand stronger because of the work that You have done in my life.

See, I have refined you, though not as silver; I have tested you in the furnace of affliction. Isaiah 48:10 NIV

So if you are suffering in a manner that pleases God, keep on doing what is right, and trust your lives to God who created you, for he will never fail you. 1 Peter 4:19 NLT

Father,

I want to thank You so much for the people that You have placed in my sons' lives to guide them and to care for them. In particular, there has been one person at church that has been so instrumental in the life of my oldest son. He has been there for him since he was a toddler. He attended Sunday School with him so that he could stay in the regular classroom, then he moved with him to the special needs' classroom. He has prayed for and encouraged my son. He attended student ministry services with him so that he could worship with other teenagers. He even baptized my son. He has shown such great love for him.

I am humbled that another person would invest so heavily in the life of my son. I know that it has happened because this man has been obedient to You and to Your call on his life. I am so thankful that he heeded Your voice. Lord, I pray that this man will know what he has meant to our son and to our entire family.

Lord, there have been many others who have spoken into the lives of my children. One of those is a sweet friend that my children call "Angel." She has been there for both of my sons since they were little boys. Her prayers for them are constant and fervent. She has been a tremendous help to me so many times by staying with my children when I had to be away from home. She cares for and loves them like they were her own family.

Lord, thank You so much for all the special people and angels that You have placed in my life and the lives of my children. I have relied on their support so much to make it this far in the journey on which You sent me.

I tell you the truth, anyone who believes in me will do the same works I have done, and even greater works because I am going to be with the Father. John 14:12 NLT

You are the light of the world—like a city on a hilltop that cannot be hidden. No one lights a lamp and then puts it under a basket. Instead, a lamp is placed on a stand, where it gives light to everyone in the house. In the same way, let your good deeds shine out for all to see, so that everyone will praise your heavenly Father. Matthew 5:14-16 NLT

Dear God,

I have cried so many tears in the past 13 years. I have cried because my children hurt. I have cried because I hurt for them. I have cried when the boys have been misunderstood, bullied, friendless, and ignored by society. I have cried when others said unkind things about them or to them. I have cried when neighbors complained about them and when other children didn't invite them to birthday parties. I have cried when school became overwhelming to them and when some teachers refused to allow them to be in their classes. I have cried when they were lonely and longing for friends. I have cried when they were angry because they just wanted to be "normal." I have cried when they became aggressive and could not control themselves. I cried because I just wanted to be a better mother, to "fix" everything, to make my children happy.

God, I am so thankful that You have seen of all my tears, that You know and understand the reason why every teardrop has fallen from my eyes. I am thankful that You keep a record of all my sorrows and that You mercifully collect all my tears in Your bottle.

You keep track of all my sorrows. You have collected all my tears in your bottle. You have recorded each one in your book. Psalm 56:8 NLT

CPSIA information can be obtained
at www.ICGtesting.com
Printed in the USA
FFOW03n0114110617
36605FF

9 781543 424270